MSU
Business
Studies

The Emergence
of Income Reporting:
An Historical Study

Brown

*The Emergence
of Income Reporting:
An Historical Study*

MSU
Business
Studies

The Emergence
of Income Reporting:
An Historical Study

Clifford D. Brown

1971
MSU Business Studies
Division of Research
Graduate School of Business Administration
Michigan State University

ISBN: 0-87744-106-5
Library of Congress Catalog Card Number: 71-634897
Copyright © 1971
By the Board of Trustees of Michigan State University
East Lansing, Michigan. All rights reserved

Printed in the United States of America

Contents

Acknowledgments

This study would not have been possible without the assistance and encouragement of many others. First of all, I wish to thank Professors Roland Salmonson, Floyd Windal, and John Henderson of the Graduate School of Business Administration, Michigan State University for their valuable comments and criticisms on the several drafts of the study. I am particularly indebted to Professor James Don Edwards, Chairman of the Department of Accounting and Financial Administration and Professor Roland I. Robinson of the same department, who were constant sources of encouragement throughout my stay at Michigan State University. Furthermore, I would like to thank Dean Jerry D. Young of the College of Business, Rochester Institute of Technology for his encouragement in converting the study to monograph form.

I also wish to acknowledge my appreciation to the American Accounting Association for its generous financial assistance during the year required for the study.

Finally, I owe my wife, Carolyn, a special debt not only for her typing and retyping of the many rough drafts, but for her patience and encouragement while at Michigan State University.

1

An Historical Approach
to Accounting

One phenomenon in the history of accounting thought is the ascendancy of the income statement to the status once held by the balance sheet as the primary accounting report. What was the nature of this ascendance? What were the underlying forces, both direct and indirect, that influenced this shift in emphasis? When did it occur? What were the contributions of various accounting writers, professional associations, governmental laws and regulations, and other persons or groups to this shift? What changes in the environment were important? What events were significant factors?

Answers to these questions are attempted in this study. It is hoped that these answers will help provide a better understanding of the relative importance of the balance sheet and income statement while demonstrating the fact that their existence is mutual and interdependent. Furthermore, such answers can provide a perspective which in turn can be utilized in analyzing and solving current problems.

LITERARY vs. SCIENTIFIC HISTORY

A literary historian writes about the grandeur of the past for its own sake. Examples of literary history in accounting are Arthur H. Woolf's *A Short History of Accountants and Accounting* and Robert H. Montgomery's *Fifty Years of Accountancy*. These works tend to reflect the grandeur of the past rather than reflecting the evolution of accounting thought, practices, and institutions in response to changing ideas and events.

The object of a scientific historian is research or inquiry aimed at discovering actions of human beings that have occurred in the past. Actions of the past are discovered not simply for their own sake, but because they provide a perspective for making wise choices today.[1] In accounting there are at least two books written to provide this perspective—A. C. Littleton and V. K. Zimmerman's *Accounting Theory: Continuity and Change* and Harvey T. Deinzer's *Development of Accounting Thought*. A quotation from Littleton and Zimmerman illustrates this scientific approach:

As a basis for an examination of the ideas behind accounting actions, it is convenient to consider first the nature and usefulness of accounting theory viewed in an historical perspective.

Behind all transmitted methods, there must have been motivating ideas. If determined, these motivating ideas of accountancy should help to explain why accounting has been able to serve so well for so many centuries and why it still shows such a remarkable capacity of growth in service potential.[2]

Similarly, a quotation from H. T. Deinzer also illustrates this approach:

The historical premise is that events are interactions; the latter have both antecedents and consequences. The more influential of the events are brought forward against a backdrop of the conditioning of environment. Further perspective may be developed by advancing certain of the characteristic events, say the "accounting events," towards the lens position, while leaving the other factors in the background as a conditioning flux.[3]

HISTORICAL METHODOLOGY

There is unanimous agreement among historians that historical methodology consists of the interpretation of evidence. But there is disagreement as to what constitutes historical evidence and how it is utilized in history.

---

[1] R. G. Collingwood, *The Idea of History*, pp. 1-2.

[2] A. C. Littleton and V. K. Zimmerman, *Accounting Theory: Continuity and Change*, p. 3.

[3] Harvey T. Deinzer, *Development of Accounting Thought*, p. 10.

Traditionally, historical evidence was that which depended upon the testimony of others.[4] Here the historian decided upon that which he wanted to know and then went to search for statements made by persons at the time of the events, or by eyewitnesses, or by repeating what eyewitnesses said, and so on for his evidence. This type of evidence is valuable to a scientific historian if it helps him to make a decision. It is useless to him if he accepts it as a ready-made answer because, by allowing someone else to make the decision for him, he is giving up his autonomy—a necessary condition for a scientific history.

This autonomous condition implies a broader definition of evidence such as that provided by Mautz and Sharaf:

> History directs its attention to the interpretation and understanding of the past by studying the influences of events and developments on the organization and behavior of human groups. Its evidence consists of documents, relics, and the written recollections and impressions of people who knew or thought they knew something about the period or event under study.[5]

Their definition describes the evidence used in this study because corporate annual reports and internal records, interviews (where appropriate), books, periodical literature, court cases, legal documents, and other sources are utilized in an effort to ascertain certain selective factors influencing the shift from the balance sheet to the income statement as the primary accounting report.

Once the question of what constitutes historical evidence has been answered, the question of how this evidence is to be utilized must be answered in order to understand the historical method. As stated earlier, consensus does not exist among historians as to the application of evidence in historical research. Irving M. Copi contends that historians must use hypotheses:

> Just as the biologist must use the method of science in formulating and testing his hypotheses, so the historian must make hypotheses, too. Even those historians who seek to limit themselves to bare descriptions of past events must work with hypotheses.[6]

Few believe that historical research involves testing hypotheses because the past has vanished, and ideas about it cannot be verified like

---

[4] Collingwood, *Idea of History*, p. 252.
[5] R. K. Mautz and Hussein A. Sharaf, *The Philosophy of Auditing*, p. 77.
[6] Irving M. Copi, *Introduction to Logic*, p. 46.

scientific hypotheses. Most believe that historical research is inferential. To quote Collingwood:

History has this in common with every other science: that the historian is not allowed to claim any single piece of knowledge, except where he can justify his claim by exhibiting to himself in the first place, and secondly to any one else who is both able and willing to follow his demonstration, the grounds upon which it is based.[7]

Furthermore, there seems to be general agreement that knowledge obtained by inference or from reasoning can only be ascertained with probability. Keynes states:

Part of our knowledge we obtain direct, and part by argument. The Theory of Probability is concerned with the part we obtained by argument....

In most branches of academic logic, such as the theory of syllogism or the geometry of ideal space, all the arguments aim at demonstrative certainty. They claim to be "conclusive." But many other arguments are rational and claim some weight without pretending to be certain. In Metaphysics, in Science, and in Conduct, most of the arguments, upon which we habitually base our rational beliefs, are admitted to be inconclusive in a greater or lesser degree. Thus for a philosophical treatment of these branches of knowledge, the study of probability is required.[8]

VALUE OF HISTORY

Joseph Schumpeter believed history has pedagogical value because it gives the student an appropriate perspective, a perspective which provides a basis for making choices today.[9]* In addition, Schumpeter thought it necessary to study the history of any subject in order to gain an awareness of the nature and speed of ideas changing within a discipline:

We learn about both the futility and fertility of controversies; about detours, wasted efforts, and blind alleys; about spells of arrested growth, about our dependence upon chance, about how not to do things, and about leeways

---

* Those who teach only from the most recent works soon find themselves in difficulty unless these works have a minimum of historical background.

[7] Collingwood, *Idea of History*, p. 252.
[8] John Maynard Keynes, *A Treatise on Probability*, p. 3.
[9] Joseph A. Schumpeter, *History of Economic Analysis*, p. 5.

to make up for. We learn to understand why we are as far as we actually are and also why we are not further.[10]

In accounting, the interaction of ideas and events make change a permanent feature. A knowledge of the nature and speed of this change places us in a better position to understand accounting's weaknesses and to see its development through time. Development of the forces shaping the change from the balance sheet to the income statement can help us discover past mistakes and give us insight into possible improvements on or alternatives to modern income reporting.

To summarize, the historical approach appropriate for this study is (1) an attempt to discover human beings' actions that have occurred in the past; (2) a process by which evidence is interpreted; and, (3) a means whereby perspective is provided for making choices today.

PROBLEMS IN STUDYING HISTORY

The historian is subject to many limitations in conducting his research. First, the raw materials at his disposal are limited. Much of the past was never recorded. In addition, that which survives today probably is distorted. This distortion is particularly true in accounting thought because its development has, historically, been dependent upon changes in practice. Unlike the history of economic thought with its long list of historical pioneers and theoretical developments, accounting thought is fragmented and only implicitly documented in the business records existing at various times. Consequently, a "considerable amount of 'pure' historical research needs to be completed in many areas prior to reaching a point at which current practices, institutions, or writings may be profitably addressed."[11]

Another limitation relates to the fact that since historical analysis is dependent mainly upon written records, bias distorts the historian's view. There is bias in the choosing of facts, bias in the organization of these facts, and ultimately bias in the interpretation of these facts.[12] The first two forms of bias can easily be overcome by explicitly re-

---

[10] Ibid., pp. 5-6.
[11] Committee Reports, *The Accounting Review* (American Accounting Association, supplement to vol. 45, 1970), p. 54.
[12] Ibid., pp. 3-9.

vealing the actual raw materials utilized, as opposed to those that were available, and by explicitly stating the organizational scheme. The former will be revealed throughout this study, whereas, the latter will be covered in the next section by reference to the approaches to the study of the history of accounting.

The third form of bias is the most complex and difficult to evaluate. It is related to whether the historian should maintain his own canons and values or should attempt to adopt those of the people and the age with which he is concerned in formulating his judgments. Few question that informed professional judgment, after a careful examination of the evidence, is an important aspect of historical research. But resultant conclusions of the historian are conditioned by influences upon his judgment. Schumpeter contended that no matter how hard we try to "cast off" those influences of our own environment we cannot succeed. Those who think they can are open to suspicion. Consequently, he recommended that our values should be clearly stated in order that others will not be misled.[13]

Schumpeter's position is also appropriate to this study. Consequently, the canons of "contemporary accounting theory" will be utilized where appropriate, although some of the theories currently being advocated are not generally accepted in accounting practice.

There is a danger in evaluating the works of earlier writers by the canons of modern day theory. Likewise, there also is a danger in ancestral worship. The former is a common occurrence for those who regard earlier works as mere rudimentary developments. On the other hand, the latter is common for those who attempt to discover in past theories an idea or concept in advance of its time. M. Blaug appropriately pointed out that, with a little training in German philosophy, these two types of dangers resemble two polar opposite positions: "relativism and absolutism."[14] The relativist regards works of the past as a reflection of the conditions of the times; the absolutist concentrates his efforts on the purely intellectual development in these earlier works in an effort to trace the progression from error to truth in the development of his discipline. Further, Blaug stated that few people ever hold strictly either of these two extreme positions but can be placed somewhere on a continuum between the poles. The absolutist's position will essentially be emphasized more in an effort

---

[13] Ibid.
[14] M. Blaug, *Economic Theory in Retrospect,* pp. 1-2.

to ascertain the relative importance of the various selective factors influencing the rise in the income statement. At the same time, however, the relativist's position will not be discarded because, as stated before, developments in accounting thought have traditionally been a function of accounting practice.

APPROACHES TO ACCOUNTING HISTORY

There are at least four approaches to the study of accounting thought, all of which involve the interpretation of evidence.

The first approach is to organize the study in terms of the dominant theme during a specific period. For example, as May suggested, accounting history could be divided into three periods according to the relative importance of the forms of business enterprises: individual ventures, either proprietorships or partnerships; corporations with limited liability owned and operated by few; and the corporation of today with the separation of owners and managers.[15] This approach is rejected for the purposes of this study because the last form—the corporation with the separation of owners and managers—was operative throughout most of the period in which the transition from the balance sheet to the income statement occurred, at least the external shift by creditors and stockholders.

A second method is to study the division of events in a chronological time sequence. An example of this approach can be found in an article by Lawrence Vance, "The Authority of History in Inventory Valuation."[16] This approach is also rejected because it generally does not focus attention upon underlying motives for accounting actions. Sequential time arrangements, although frequently a necessary condition, should not be the basic object in a study of the history of accounting thought.

A third approach is to organize one's findings in such a way as to present a story. As mentioned earlier, examples of this approach are numerous in accounting and have little value because emphasis is placed upon recreating the spectacle of the past rather than upon reasons behind accounting actions of the past.

---

[15] George O. May, *Financial Accounting*, p. 51.
[16] Lawrence Vance, "The Authority of History in Inventory Valuation," *Accounting Review*, July 1943, pp. 218-27.

The last important possible approach is to determine the inter-relationships between ideas and events—both endogenous and exogenous. Why did certain ideas originate? To what extent did events influence the development of these ideas? This approach is usually the best because it enables the researcher to relate the environment to changing ideas and concepts. It will be the approach generally followed in this study since the effects of environmental change provided the seeds that resulted in the shift in emphasis from the balance sheet to the income statement.

2

The Internal Shift from
Balance Sheet to Income Statement

Before the advent of the corporate form of business organization, the era when owner and manager were identical, and when business income or profits resulted from successful ventures or from monopoly power, it was "unlikely that annual income statements were of use for the purpose of testing the profitability of operations as a whole as a guide to future action."[1] On the other hand, the balance sheet was of considerable importance during this early era. For example, Littleton suggested that in the fifteenth century the balance sheet reflected a merchant's "estate" for property tax purposes. In addition, he referred to the French ordinance ("Inventaire") proposed by Jacques Savary in 1673 and to other early examples which show the balance sheet as the "estate" and the income statement simply as "proof of the estate."[2] These examples of early practices suggest that the balance sheet was accorded superiority over the income statement by both internal users and external parties.

But today, the opposite is the case and income statement data are considered more important. Thus, there was a shift in emphasis from the balance sheet viewpoint to the profit and loss viewpoint. In fact,

---

[1] Raymond J. Chambers, "The Implications of Asset Revaluation and Bonus Share Issues," p. 514.
[2] A. C. Littleton, *Accounting Evolution to 1900,* pp. 132-36.

there is evidence that suggests that there was a dual shift; there was a shift to the use of income data by management and there was a shift by investors, creditors, and other external interested parties. This chapter will discuss the former shift not only because it occurred first chronologically, but because it was one of the forces responsible for the latter shift in interest.

THE NEW EMPHASIS ON PROFITS

BEGINNINGS OF INDUSTRIALIZATION

The numerous inventions in England between 1750 and 1800 are important events because they ushered in what has been called the Industrial Revolution. English economic society needed only a slight stimulant to crystallize in a new form, and the stimulant came from inventions in the textile industry in response to the rapidly increasing foreign and domestic demand for goods and services. The inventive genius of James Hargreaves in his spinning jenny (1764), Richard Arkwright in his water frame (1769), Samuel Crompton in his spinning mule (1779), and John Kay (1738) and Edmund Cartwright (1784) in their perfection of power weaving introduced mechanical inventions that made possible the production of a greatly increased quantity of goods through the use of the factory system. In addition, the improvement of the steam engine by James Watt (1785) was also a milestone because it enabled the supplanting of power provided by animals.[3] Although these inventions and improvements had substantial impacts on all subsequent aspects of economic activity and were themselves the result of many complex and remote causes, their immediate impact on the internal shift in emphasis from the balance sheet to the income statement point of view is minimal because the proprietorship and partnership forms of business organizations still dominated. As a result, owners were generally managers who had no reason for testing the profitability of operations as a whole as a guide to future action. Nevertheless, there were scattered developments in cost accounting during this period which indicate that a change was

---

[3] Edward McNall Burns, *Western Civilizations,* pp. 636-42.

in the making.[4] In addition, there were signs that the rise of the factory system would eventually require a new form of business organization—the corporation. Particularly, the main signs were the large capital investments that were beginning to be needed and the increasingly competitive environment making survival tenuous at best.

THE SECOND INDUSTRIAL REVOLUTION

The Industrial Revolution in approximately 1860 entered a new phase so different from what had preceded it that some historians call it the Second Industrial Revolution. The events which ushered in this new phase were mainly the Bessemer process for making steel, the perfection of the dynamo, and the invention of the internal combustion engine.[5] These and other events resulted in the development of an industrial society based on technology, mass production, and mass marketing. A system based on partnerships or joint-stock companies emerged in America and has been called *industrial capitalism*. The great industrial capitalists, such as Andrew Carnegie, Samuel Slater, Philip Armour, and Gordon McKay, were specialists in production rather than finance and followed a social code from the philosophy of Social Darwinism. This code held that economic life, like biological life, was the survival of the fittest. Professor Herman Kroose's remarks about the industrial capitalist are particularly significant:

Usually starting on a small scale, he raised most of his capital by plowing earnings back into his business. He despised financial mechanisms, such as balance sheets, income statements, and value based on earnings, and drew no distinction between the stockholder and the speculator.[6]

In the quest of increased supply of goods through the principle of survival of the fittest, the industrial capitalist naturally placed emphasis on efficiency as measured by the volume of output (for example, tons of steel). These men concentrated on dynamic individuals

---

[4] For a good summary of these developments see S. Paul Garner, "Highlights in the Development of Cost Accounting," reprinted in *Readings in Cost Accounting, Budgeting and Control*, 2d ed., ed., William E. Thomas, Jr. (New Rochelle, N.Y.: South-Western Publishing Company, 1960), pp. 2-14.

[5] Burns, *Western Civilizations*, p. 643.

[6] Herman E. Kroose, *American Economic Development*, p. 275.

placed in the right jobs and encouraged rivalries between managers and superintendents in an effort to squeeze even greater efforts. They generally did not believe in "evaluating a business on the basis of its earning power."[7] Thus, they did not concentrate on income statement data or elaborate cost accounting systems. Nevertheless, their emphasis on efficiency was to continue into the corporation; but profitability became the method of its measurement.

RISE OF THE CORPORATIONS

By 1890 the state of technological progress and the growing consumer demand for mass-produced goods required large amounts of capital. Furthermore, the bitterly competitive atmosphere that the great industrial capitalists had created with their ruthless tactics resulted in a high bankruptcy rate and a high degree of insecurity among average businessmen. As a result, there was a need for a type of business organization that would provide the necessary capital and yet reduce the high degree of personal liability.

The corporate form of business organization, although legally sanctioned much earlier,[8] was ideally suited to fulfill these two needs through its stock ownership, limited liability, transferability of interests, and separation of owners and managers features. The individual generally considered responsible for the initiation of this corporate revolution in America was the so-called financial capitalist[9]

---

[7] Ibid., p. 276.

[8] The first modern corporation law in the United States was passed by the Connecticut legislature in 1837, although New York State had passed a less modern version in 1811. The first modern corporation act in England was the British Companies Act in 1862, although a less complete act was passed in 1855.

[9] J. Pierpont Morgan was the chief representative of the new financial capitalists. For a good discussion of his exploits see Lewis Corey, *The House of Morgan*. For example, he became the head railroad financier in 1879 when he handled the sale of 250,000 shares of New York Central stock; in 1892 he helped organize the General Electric Company; in 1901 his capital consolidated firms producing 60 percent of the nation's steel into the U.S. Steel Corporation; also he was an important factor behind the establishment of American Telephone and Telegraph Company, International Harvester, as well as holding a controlling interest in a number of commercial banks, trust companies, and insurance companies.

—the banker, the investment banker, and the insurance company.

The business policies of the financial capitalists were quite different from the industrial capitalists. They tended to spread their influence over many different industries instead of specializing in a single business. Consequently, the financial capitalists were instrumental in many reorganizations and consolidations. As a result, their interests were too diversified to permit them to undertake an active entrepreneurial role in the actual day-to-day decision making of a business and managers were appointed to assume this function. This delegation of authority to management eventually resulted in the emergence of a new force, the professional managerial class.[10]

As might be expected, financial capitalists were more interested in financial policy than in any other aspect of business activity. They preferred corporate finance rather than industrial management as the following quotation reveals:

Income statements and balance sheets, earnings per share, security prices, capitalization and security flotations interested them much more than the index of industrial production, the output of pig iron, or the volume of car loadings.[11]

Although the financial capitalists were important factors contributing to the internal shift in emphasis, as is obvious from their financial policies, it was the new professional managerial class resulting from the corporate form of business organization that was really important.

The ascendancy of the professional manager, like all changes in business history, was not a revolutionary change. It took place gradually and reflected among other things the government's increasing economic influence evidenced by the antitrust legislation, the increasing importance of labor unions, and public concern over the standard of living.[12] The most important factor, however, was the increasing complexity of the business enterprise itself. Stockholders were becoming so numerous and businesses so large and complex that it became impracticable for owners to both control and operate their corporations. Thus it became feasible for a group of professionals,

---

[10] E. A. Johnson and Herman E. Kroose, *The American Economy,* pp. 250-54.

[11] Ibid., p. 251.

[12] Ibid., p. 261.

who were specialists, to make the necessary decisions. No single individual possessed the breadth of knowledge, time, or energy to make all the decisions of a large corporation. In short, the directors of a large corporation had "to use accounting and statistics; the management had to be departmentalized; and experts in each field became important."[13]

Among other things, the two more important impacts on accounting thought and practice at first were the need to test the profitability of operations through the use of cost and revenue data by the professional managers and the emphasis on the balance sheet for external parties to meet the demands of the auditors, owners, and the financial capitalists, particularly banks. This latter phenomenon was enhanced because of the widespread fear that legislation requiring the presentation of audited balance sheets, such as the Joint Stock Companies Act of 1862 in England, would also appear in the United States. For example, Section 94 of this British act stated that the auditors must disclose "whether in their opinion the balance sheet is a full and fair balance sheet."[14] On the other hand, there were no pressures demanding the disclosure of income statement data in the early years of the corporate form of business organization. In fact, it was the general belief that profit and loss data were confidential information that could, if disclosed, aid competitors. As a result, income statements that provided any meaningful information were seldom released.

EVIDENCE OF THE INTERNAL SHIFT

DEVELOPMENT OF COST ACCOUNTING

One of the most significant developments that provides evidential support for the internal shift in emphasis was the rapid emergence of cost accounting between 1885 and 1930. One of the earliest works in this area was Henry Metcalfe's *Cost of Manufactures,* first published in 1885. Although many of the ideas and techniques suggested by Metcalfe were not unknown, their integration into a unified costing sys-

---

[13] Ibid., pp. 262-63.

[14] A. C. Littleton and V. K. Zimmerman, *Accounting Theory: Continuity and Change,* p. 106.

tem was a significant accomplishment because the beginnings of cost control for profit improvement were introduced.[15]

Two years after the first edition of Metcalfe's book appeared, two English practicing cost accountants, M. Garcke and G. Fells, published the first edition of their book *Factory Accounts*. Despite the fact that they introduced a scheme for showing the flow of cost through the firm that resembled today's method, the most striking innovation was their procedure for integrating cost accounts with financial accounts in the general ledger.[16] From this procedure it was a simple task to use revenue accounts and cost accounts for the calculation of profit and loss from operation.

American writers quickly espoused this idea of integrating cost and financial accounts. For example, in expanding on a series of articles by A. Hamilton Church, John Whitmore implied the new emphasis on profits in the following quotation:

The fundamental principle is always the same, namely the principle of making a record sufficiently full to constitute a clear accounting for factory expenditure; and the object of the accounts is always the same, namely, to eliminate waste from operations.[17]

Furthermore, in commenting on the relationship of factory accounting to managerial organization he stated:

The organization of a factory and its system of accounts and records are so closely allied, are so inseparable, that to talk of one is necessarily to talk of the other.[18]

After detailing his cost system and the necessary journal entries to integrate it into the financial accounts, Whitmore explained, "Profits are determined on the basis of these cost figures . . . giving thus the net result of operations."[19] These quotations indicate it was recognized that the integration of cost accounts into financial accounts made possible an improved method for calculating profit and loss through the matching of revenues and expenses.

---

[15] Garner, "Development of Cost Accounting," in *Readings in Cost Accounting, Budgeting and Control*, pp. 9-10.

[16] S. Paul Garner, *Evolution of Cost Accounting to 1925*, p. 257.

[17] John Whitmore, "Factory Accounts as Applied to Machine Shops," p. 249.

[18] Ibid., p. 345.

[19] Ibid., vol. 3 (November 1906), p. 31.

Other writers followed Whitmore's idea of account integration while stressing the importance of cost accounting for profit improvement through cost control. J. Lee Nicholson treated the matter at length in several of his books—*Factory Organization and Costs* (1909), *Cost Accounting-Theory and Practice* (1913), *Cost Accounting,* with J. D. Rohrback (1919), and *Profitable Management* (1923). Nicholson's 1909 publication was important because he emphasized what we would call today a cost center where costs were to be accumulated under the three main elements, direct labor, materials, and burden. But, most importantly, he introduced a system of distinguishing the sales for each division or department so that gross profit calculations could be made by division or department.[20] The significance of this development is that it provides further evidence of the extent to which income statement data were being utilized internally. In his 1913 work Nicholson elaborated on the ideas and methods contained in his first book and also presented an elaborate procedure for coordinating the cost and financial ledgers through the use of two reciprocal accounts.[21]

Although Nicholson's 1919 and 1923 books refined and elaborated his earlier publications, several quotations indicate the importance accorded income and expense data. These quotations also show that the integration of cost and financial accounts was complete. The former is illustrated when he stated:

The methods of modern business have become exceedingly technical and complex. But their objective is easy to define—it is control of the business; and control is wanted to insure profits.[22]

Account integration is suggested in the following:

Cost accounting, as a science, is a branch of general accounting . . . . With the cost books once established, the best modern usage is to incorporate their record in total in the general financial books. In this way the modern cost system builds up an interworking series of accounts which furnish the basis for a detailed study of the operations of a manufacturing business.[23]

Other American writers such as Frank E. Webner and C. E. Knoeppel, the engineer-accountant, were also espousing ideas and concepts

---

[20] J. Lee Nicholson, *Factory Organization and Costs,* pp. 31-33.
[21] See S. Paul Garner, *Evolution,* p. 271.
[22] J. Lee Nicholson, *Profitable Management,* preface.
[23] J. Lee Nicholson and John F. D. Rohrback, *Cost Accounting,* p. 5.

similar to Nicholson. Webner stated, "the slogan of present-day industry is efficiency."[24] He also felt that cost accounts and general accounts should be integrated.[25] In describing the relationship between accounting and engineering C. E. Knoeppel stated:

Accounting and engineering are concerned with the same thing—reducing costs—for only through a reduction of costs can larger profits or increased margin of sales be expected.[26]

It is also worth mentioning the cost convention, as W. A. Paton called it, that became a basic assumption in cost accounting. This convention is important because it became integrated into the matching concept as its characteristics indicate. A quotation from Stephen Gilman makes this point clear:

This new subdivision of accounting (cost convention) was based upon a convention that costs could be transferred from one object to another, from one classification to another, and from one activity to another. Thus, the depreciation of a building operates as a transfer of value from the building itself to the materials in progress of manufacture, simultaneously lessening one value and increasing another.

This convention enables the cost accountant to visualize a flow of values springing from expenditures of various types, through classified channels, finally attaching themselves to, and increasing the valuation of, the materials in process of manufacture. Direct labor and various other factory costs, such as rent, heat, light, property taxes, insurance, and supervision, came to be regarded as assets because they attach themselves to materials in process.[27]

This convention is important because it attempted to show a direct relationship between specific items of income and specific items of cost-outlay. The lacking element for the matching concept was the identification of the items to specific time periods.

ACTIVITIES OF THE SCIENTIFIC MANAGEMENT ENGINEERS

The activities of the so-called scientific management engineers, al-

---

[24] Frank E. Webner, *Factory Costs*, p. 25.
[25] Ibid., p. 29.
[26] C. E. Knoeppel, *Organization and Administration*, p. 245.
[27] Stephen Gilman, *Accounting Concepts of Profit*, p. 29.

though not a direct indication of the shift by management to income statement data, provide indirect evidence of the new emphasis. This evidence is revealed throughout their writings by the emphasis accorded efficiency of operations, which in turn, implied a new emphasis on profits. For example, Frederick W. Taylor, considered the father of scientific management, stated:

The principal object of management should be to secure the maximum prosperity for the employer, coupled with the maximum prosperity for each employee.[28]

He also used the words "maximum prosperity" in their broad sense to mean not only large dividends for the firm or owner, but the development of every branch of business to its highest state of excellence, so that prosperity may be permanent.[29]

In a more technical book, *Shop Management,* Taylor turned to or worked directly with cost accountants as a means of measuring efficiency. Cost accounting techniques were used to compare the actual cost of an operation to its predetermined cost. This comparison was actually the beginning of standard costs where the difference between standard and actual cost could be used as a basis for investigating waste and inefficiency. Taylor believed this method of measuring efficiency represented the principle of scientific management—"knowing exactly what you want men to do, and then seeing they do it in the best and cheapest way."[30]

Another American engineer, Henry L. Gantt, concentrated his efforts on the matter of idle time and capacity by proposing that indirect expenses chargeable to output of the factory should bear the same ratio as those chargeable at normal capacity. In short, he was introducing the present notion of "normal" burden and predetermined overhead rates. This emphasis on overhead costs and Taylor's use of elementary standard costing is important because it helped provide a means for a better matching of revenues and expenses. As a result, the utility of the income statement was enhanced.[31]

There were many other scientific management engineers whose efforts are indicative of the fact that an internal shift to profit and loss

---

[28] Frederick W. Taylor, *The Principles of Scientific Management,* p. 9.
[29] Ibid.
[30] Frederick W. Taylor, *Shop Management,* p. 21.
[31] Eldon S. Hendrickson, *Accounting Theory,* pp. 30-31.

data had occurred. For the purposes of this study, reference to an article by C. Bertrand Thompson is sufficient to demonstrate this shift, even though these scientific management engineers were not specifically concerned with the accounting problems associated with the matching process.

The development of the factory system brought with it many new problems connected with the organization and labor, the structure and equipment of factories, and the techniques of production. By successful manufactures these problems have always been solved in a way to make manufacturing at a profit possible. Early solutions, however, were necessarily crude and roughshod. With the enormous increase in demand for manufactured products, in the investment of capital, and the number of men engaged in business, with the consequent development of ever-keener competition the early methods have been found insufficient. Especially within the last twenty years a degree of skill and technical training has been brought to bear upon the solution of factory problems which has made modern factory management much more elaborate, refined, and effective than ever before.[32]

EVIDENCE FROM SELECTED FIRMS

Developments in cost accounting and the activities of the scientific management engineers provide a certain kind of documentation for the new emphasis on profits because the techniques, procedures, and theories proposed were all geared to cost reduction for increased efficiency of operations, which in turn, would hopefully result in increased profits. In essence, one might postulate that the most logical reason for these developments and activities was the increased demand for information by management resulting from the rise of the corporate organization, the increased size and complexity of business, and the changing competitive environment which evolved from the industrialization of society. Even though the literature of the cost accounting and scientific management writers is highly suggestive of the internal shift in emphasis, it is not conclusive enough to conform with the requirements of "scientific" historical research as suggested in chapter one. Thus, as part of the research for this study an attempt was made to secure early internal income statements to ascertain whether income data were actually emphasized before the shift from

---

[32] C. Bertrand Thompson, "The Literature of Scientific Management," p. 506.

the balance sheet to the income statement occurred for external parties
in the early 1930s.

The investigation conducted started with the selection of forty-five
businesses, shown in Illustration I, which were listed on the New

ILLUSTRATION I
LIST OF SELECTED COMPANIES CONTACTED

1. Allied Chemical Corporation
2. Allis-Chalmers Company
3. American Can Company
4. American Ship Building Company
5. American Smelting & Refining Company
6. American Steel Foundries, Inc.
7. American Telephone & Telegraph Company
8. Anaconda Company
9. Armour and Company
10. B. F. Goodrich Company
11. Bethlehem Steel Corporation
12. Brunswick Corporation
13. Coca-Cola Company
14. Crucible Steel Company of America
15. E. I. duPont deNémours and Company
16. Eastman Kodak Company
17. F. W. Woolworth Company
18. General Electric Company
19. General Motors Company
20. International Harvester Company
21. J. C. Penney Company, Inc.
22. Kellogg Company
23. Kennecott Corporation
24. Liggett & Myers Tobacco, Inc.
25. National Biscuit Company
26. National Steel Corporation
27. New York Air Brake Company
28. Otis Elevator Company
29. Owens-Illinois
30. Phelps Dodge Corporation
31. Procter & Gamble Company
32. Pullman Incorporated
33. P. Lorillard Company
34. Remington Office Equipment
35. Republic Steel Company
36. S. S. Kresge Company
37. Sears, Roebuck & Company
38. Sinclair Oil Corporation
39. Standard Oil Company of New Jersey
40. U.S. Rubber Company (Uniroyal)
41. United Fruit Company
42. United States Envelope Company
43. United States Steel Corporation
44. Westinghouse Electric Company
45. White Motor Corporation

York Stock Exchange on or before 1920 (twenty-five were listed in
1912) and which still survive. The governing factor in the selection
process was survival of the firm today so that the desired information
could be more readily obtained. On the other hand, companies were

selected from various industries so that a cross section of data could be obtained in order to indicate the scope of internal statement used before 1930. Although a statistically testable sample was not drawn, the selection was appropriate because the number of corporations listed on the New York Stock Exchange in 1920 or before was relatively small as compared to today.

The second step was to mail a copy of the letter shown in Illustration II to the controllers of each of the previously listed forty-five

ILLUSTRATION II

SAMPLE COPY OF LETTER MAILED TO
FORTY-FIVE SELECTED COMPANIES

Mr. James Jones
Vice President and Comptroller
XYZ Corporation
1690 Erie Road
Pittsburgh, Pennsylvania 15230

Dear Mr. Jones:

As a doctor of philosophy candidate in accounting I am writing my dissertation in the area of the history of accounting thought. Specifically, this study will be concerned with the shift in emphasis from the balance sheet to the income statement as the primary accounting report.

Since the XYZ Corporation was a pioneer in the development of annual reporting to stockholders, your old statements are an invaluable aid. However, it seems necessary to ascertain whether or not an elaborate income statement was prepared internally, as opposed to the condensed version for external reporting, before the shift in emphasis occurred during the early 1930s. If there were elaborate income statements prepared at this time, I would very much appreciate a copy of one or a visit to your company to examine them if they are unavailable.

Thank you for your anticipated cooperation.

Sincerely yours,
Clifford D. Brown
Doctoral Candidate
Michigan State University

companies asking for internal income statements for a period before the external shift from the balance sheet to the income statement as the primary accounting report occurred during the early 1930s. Of the forty-five companies receiving letters, nine did not reply and eight either stated that for one reason or another their records did not extend back to that era or their company's policy did not permit them to divulge such information. The remaining twenty-eight companies that did reply sent copies of early internal income statements, disclosed their nature in a letter, or included combinations of both.

Upon analyzing these internal statements and letters it was concluded that income statement data were highly significant for internal management long before the shift in emphasis occurred for external parties, such as investors and creditors. These statements and letters do not, however, specifically document a shift from balance sheet data to income statement data by internal management. They simply suggest that no shift occurred internally during the early 1930s, the time that, as will be shown later, it occurred in the minds of external parties. The latter suggestion is particularly important to this study even though as was suggested earlier, there is reason to believe that the rise of the corporation in response to the changing economic scene resulted in the increased emphasis on profit and loss data by internal management between 1890 and 1930. A documentation of the fact that profit and loss data were extensively used by management before 1930 is sufficient evidence to conclude that the shift in emphasis from the balance sheet to the income statement in the 1930s as the primary accounting report was an external shift only. On the other hand, this conclusion does not preclude the suggestion that the external shift did not have an impact on internal accounting. To be sure, the refinement of the matching concept and the resulting principles underlying the preparation of financial statements that resulted from this new external emphasis on the income statement affected internal accounting by providing better techniques and methods for the assembly and communication of more relevant and timely information.

Some selected quotations and examples from these replies support the above conclusion. John N. Hart, vice president and controller of B. F. Goodrich Company, in his letter of November 28, 1967 said:

The shift in emphasis, which you are concerned with, is a shift made by creditors and stockholders who are outside the business as compared to internal operating people who are concerned with the day-to-day problems of production and sales.

Furthermore, he stated in reference to internal balance sheets prior to 1930 "that very few operating personnel below the senior corporate executive received balance sheets." On the other hand, in regard to internal income statements of this early era he stated that they "varied in degree of 'elaborateness' depending upon the level of management to which they were furnished."

G. D. Dearlove, assistant comptroller of International Harvester Company, commented on his company's internal income statements prior to 1930:

While there have been changes in philosophy and improvements in format over the years, internal income statements of the Company have always been in sufficient detail to provide adequate information for internal management purposes and, therefore, of necessity, have generally been more complete than statements appropriate for external reporting.

Fillmore B. Eisenberg, vice president and controller of the Coca-Cola Company, wrote regarding the form of his company's internal income statement prior to the 1930s:

... for internal management purposes we have always prepared more detailed statements than those published in the annual reports to stockholders. Over the years these statements have taken various forms and emphasis has been directed to different areas depending on the nature of conditions and problems extant at the time, since as you know our Company has developed greatly and in many directions over its long history. Our objective with regard to internal management statements has always been to supply operating managers with sufficient detail, either in the income statements, or as supporting schedules to allow them to have a comprehensive picture of current operations. Such information would in general consist of sales, both dollars and units of product, details of manufacturing expenses and other cost of sales items and details of various operating expenses.

Charles C. Link, Jr., assistant comptroller of American Smelting and Refining Company wrote in reference to his company's internal income statements before 1930:

In connection with your recent letter concerning income statements prior to the 1930's, you are correct in your assumption that ASARCO prepared for internal use a more detailed income statement than that used in its external reporting.

Basically, the Company philosophy has always been oriented toward reporting earnings by management responsibility. Each plant or mine is treated as an individual profit center, and an individual profit and loss statement is prepared by each (generally on a monthly basis). This was true even before 1930.

The internal income statement before 1930 included three main groups: smelting and refining plants, mines, and all other items. Each plant and mine was listed and the total earnings of each group reported. The plants were the responsibility of the Vice-President in charge of Smelting and Refining, while the mines were the responsibility of the Vice-President in the Mining Department. Each of these vice-presidents had group managers in turn responsible for certain subdivisions (Mexican smelters, Mexican mines, Southwestern Mining Departments, etc.).

The "all other items," which were small in number, were the responsibility of other Company officials although not then important enough to be reported in sub-groups.

This early basic system is still in use today, but it has been expanded to reflect larger volume of business and the importance of additional activities now performed by the Company.

N. E. Jones, associate comptroller of the Procter & Gamble Company, commented:

Income statements prepared for internal use prior to 1930 were just as elaborate and detailed as those prepared after the shift in emphasis occurred during the early 1930's. Our perusal of the available internal records in the 20's and 30's shows no shift in emphasis or detail. The change which occurred was an external change.

An executive of a large steel company answered in his letter:

In both the period prior to the early 1930's and the current period there are detailed supporting statements for internal use—many more now than in the early period due to the decentralization of management and the general trend to responsibility accounting at all levels. The availability of data processing equipment serves these needs but additionally provides more detail which could not have been provided under the essentially manual techniques employed in the earlier years.

E. A. Bescherer, specialist—General Accounting Research, of the General Electric Company stated:

A review of our reports at that time indicates that there were more elaborate reports prepared internally from at least the mid-1900's. For example, for 1930 a statement was prepared which analyzed operating results down through "Profits available for dividends" by major segments of the business. In addition, there were more detailed breakdowns of a number of the items, such as "Income from other sources," shown in the published statements.

This statement by Bescherer is supported and documented in a series of three books entitled *General Electric's Growth, General Electric's*

Organization, and *The Work of a Professional Manager,* copyrighted by the General Electric Company under the title *Professional Management in General Electric.*[33]

F. G. Saviers, assistant controller of Westinghouse Electric Corporation, stated that "in the year 1928 the corporate statement (income) included considerably more detail than that which was published in the Annual Report." To verify this he included a copy of the income statement and a copy of the internal income statement for the same year. These statements are reproduced in Illustration III and Illustration IV. Furthermore, he felt that "there were many detailed state-

ILLUSTRATION III

WESTINGHOUSE ELECTRIC STATEMENT OF CONSOLIDATED INCOME AND PROFIT & LOSS FOR THE YEAR ENDED MARCH 31, 1928

Gross Earnings		
Sales billed		xxxx
Cost of Sales:		
Factory cost, including depreciation of property and plant and all distribution, administration, and general expenses; and taxes		xxxx
Net Manufacturing Profit		xxxx
Other Income:		
Interest, discount, and miscellaneous income and profits	xxxx	
Dividends and interest on sundry stocks and bonds owned	xxxx	xxxx
Gross Income from All Sources		xxxx
Deductions from Income:		
Interest charges		xxxx
Net Income for the Year		xxxx
Dividends on Preferred and Common Stocks		xxxx
Surplus for the Year		xxxx
Surplus, March 31, 1927		xxxx

[33] See for example chapter two, "Evolution of Organization," in book one, *General Electric's Growth,* pp. 23-58.

ILLUSTRATION III (continued)

Gross Surplus   xxxx
Adjustments:
  Reserves for possible adjustments of book values of
    investments in affiliated companies, for pensions
    and for notes and accounts receivable and mis-
    cellaneous charges, less profit realized on the sale
    of certain investments   xxxx
  Patents, charters, franchises, and so forth, written
    down to nominal value   xxxx
                   Total   xxxx
  Less balance of reserve previously appropriated for
    federal income taxes, not required   xxxx   xxxx
Surplus, March 31, 1928, Per Balance Sheet   xxxx

ILLUSTRATION IV

WESTINGHOUSE ELECTRIC COMPARATIVE STATEMENT OF OPERATIONS FOR THE PERIOD ENDED MARCH 31, 1928

Net sales billed   xxxx
Cost of sales billed   xxxx
  Percentage of net sales billed   xxxx
Manufacturing profit   xxxx
General expenses:
  Distribution   xxxx
  Administration   xxxx
                   Total   xxxx
Gross operating profit   xxxx
  Percentage of net sales billed   xxxx
Other charges against operations   xxxx
  Miscellaneous charges   xxxx
  Standard development—unapplied   xxxx
                   Total   xxxx
Net operating profit   xxxx
  Percentage of net sales billed   xxxx
Other income:
  From investments   xxxx

ILLUSTRATION IV (continued)

Dividends—other proprietary companies	xxxx	
Interest and discount	xxxx	
Royalties	xxxx	
Miscellaneous	xxxx	
Total		xxxx
Gross income (line 13 plus 20)	xxxx	
Deductions from income:		
Interest charges	xxxx	
Federal taxes accrued and miscellaneous	xxxx	
Total		xxxx
Net income	xxxx	
Surplus adjustments, net	xxxx	
Intermanufacturing company dividends	xxxx	
Surplus for period	xxxx	
Surplus beginning of period	xxxx	
Surplus available for dividends and other purposes	xxxx	
Dividends on capital stock:		
Preferred stock	xxxx	
Common stock	xxxx	
Total		xxxx
Surplus end of period		xxxx

ments prepared for internal use for such items of expense as distribution, administration, etc." even though, in accordance with company policy, these detailed statements were not retained. At a glance, one of the significant features of the internal income statement, or the comparative statement of operations as it is called, was the separation of manufacturing profit expressed both in dollars and as percentages of net sales billed. On the other hand, in the published statement of consolidated income and profit and loss, these items were included in one figure, the cost of sales, leaving a net manufacturing profit balance. These alternative treatments suggest the importance given to profit and loss data for internal purposes as opposed to the condensed version for external purposes prior to the occurrence of the so-called shift in emphasis in the early 1930s.

F. L. Linton, assistant comptroller of Allied Chemical Corporation, stated in his reply that:

Allied Chemical was organized in 1920 by the alliance of five companies which subsequently became operating divisions. The income statements prepared for the managements of these companies and the consolidated income statement were much more detailed than the published condensed version.

Another major supporting schedule presented sales quantities, sales dollars, cost of sales and gross profit by major products or major product groups.

He also included selected copies of the company's methods bulletin which showed the composition of the internal income statement and the major supporting schedules of expenses used prior to the 1930s. (These copies are shown in Illustration V.) From the detail of the

ILLUSTRATION V

ALLIED CHEMICAL & DYE CORPORATION
METHODS BULLETIN IN USE BEFORE 1930

Sales
  Sales—domestic
  Sales—export-direct and foreign
    (102) Sales—export-direct
    (103) Sales—export-foreign
      branches
  Total sales
  Discounts
  Sales—net
  Cost of sales
  Gross profit
Deductions from Gross Profit
  Selling expense
  General administration expense
  Freight car operations—net
  Marine equipment operations—
    net
  Idle plant expense
  Miscellaneous
  Other deductions
Operating Profit
Other Income
  Interest
  Dividends
  Commissions and brokerage—net
  Operating contracts—net
  Discount on purchases
  Barrett Building and other
    rentals—net

Other Income (continued)
    (120) Rentals—net
    (122) Barrett Building
      Company—net
  Miscellaneous
    Engineering and other
    services rendered—net
  Tully Farms operations
Gross Income
Deductions from Gross Income
  Federal and Canadian income
    taxes
      (126) Federal income taxes
      (127) Canadian income taxes
  Interest
      (128) Interest on funded debt
      (129) Other interest
  Bad debts reserve
  Miscellaneous
      (130) Minority interests
Net Income
Surplus at Beginning
Surplus Adjustment
  Surplus adjustment—credit
  Surplus adjustment—debit
Deductions from Surplus
  Dividends—preferred
  Dividends—common
Surplus—Balance Sheet

ILLUSTRATION V *(continued)*

List of Manufacturing Cost Controlling Accounts

Raw and productive materials
    consumed
Productive labor
Manufacturing expense
    Fuel
    Manufacturing supplies
    Maintenance
    Power
    Plant transportation
    Warehousing

Tests and inspection
Research and development
Plant administration
Depreciation
Dismantling and retirements
Insurance—other than fire
Insurance—fire
Taxes
Other manufacturing expenses
By-products and residuals

ALLIED CHEMICAL & DYE CORPORATION
SELLING EXPENSE CLASSIFICATION SHOWING THE GROUPING
OF SELLING EXPENSE ACCOUNTS

Classification
Salaries:
  Managers and salesmen
  Office employees
  Warehouse employees
  Mixing department employees
  Laboratory employees
  Other employees
Expenses of Employees:
  Managers and salesmen
  Other employees
Office Operating Expense:
  Supplies and incidental expense,
    office and warehousing
  Supplies and incidental expense,
    laboratory
  Stationery and printing
  Postage
  Telephone, telegraph,
    and cable
  Light, heat, and power
Building and Equipment
Expense:
  Repairs and renewals—
    buildings
  Repairs and renewals—
    office equipment
  Repairs and renewals—
    other equipment

  Depreciation—buildings and
    office and other equipment
  Rent of offices and buildings
Brokerage
Storage
Advertising:
  Samples
  Advertising
  Newspapers, periodicals,
    and exhibits
  Circulars and catalogues
Classification
Containers, Packages, and
Packing Material
Freight and Express:
  Freight and express—
    inward
  Freight and express—
    outward
Trucking and Drayage:
  Trucking employees
  Supplies and expenses
  Repairs and renewals—
    trucking
  Depreciation—
    trucking
  Insurance—trucking
  Taxes—trucking
  Drayage

ILLUSTRATION V (continued)

Insurance and Taxes:
Insurance—other
Taxes—other
Other Expenses:
Bank exchange and
collection fees
Profit and loss on
foreign exchange
Bad debts collection

expenses
Amortization of leasehold
expenditures
Export charges
Custom duties
Barrett specification
inspection
Other expenses

Allied Chemical & Dye Corporation
General Administration Expense Classification Showing the Grouping of General Administration Expense Accounts

Classification
Salaries:
Officials and department
heads
Clerks and attendants
Engineers
Chemists
Office building employees
Expenses of Employees:
Transportation and
pullman fares
Other expenses
Entertainment
*Law Expenses and Special
Services:*
Trademark and patent
expense
Law expense
Special services
Office Operating Expense:
Stationery and printing
Telephone, telegraph, and
cable service
Postage
Incidental expense
Light, heat, and power
Office supplies
Classification
Building and Equipment Expenses:
Rent of offices and
buildings

Depreciation of buildings
Depreciation of
equipment
Amortization of leasehold
expenditures
Repairs and renewals—
equipment
Repairs and renewals—
buildings
Rental of office
equipment
*Contributions, Subscriptions,
and Memberships:*
Selling expense
General administration
expense
Insurance and Taxes:
Fire insurance
Employer's liability
insurance
Other insurance
State income taxes
Other taxes
Pensions
Other Expenses:
Domestic exchange
Foreign exchange—net
Royalties
Other expenses

items under income and surplus classification, the list of manufacturing cost controlling accounts, selling expense classification, and the general administration expense, one is led to believe that profit and loss data were extensively utilized for both planning and controlling of operations before the 1930s. Thus, as with the preceding examples, no significant shift from the balance sheet to the income statement occurred internally during the 1930s.

T. A. Murphy, comptroller of General Motors Corporation, likewise stated in his reply:

The scope of internal income reporting has not changed appreciably since the early 1920's. We have, of course, made improvements in reporting techniques but, for the most part, these improvements have principally tended to reduce the great volume of data which formerly was reported to management in order to tell the financial story in as concise a manner as possible. Significant financial reports which were prepared in this early period, as well as today, included the forecast income statement and financial budgets. These financial tools, which are commonplace now with most companies, were not so widely used by other concerns at that time. However, in General Motors, it could be fairly stated that increasing emphasis has been placed on forward estimates rather than historical data.

As to our published financial statements, you may also find it interesting to note that since 1923 the income statement has preceded the balance sheet in the annual report to the stockholders of the Corporation.

This statement can further be verified by reference to the work of Alfred P. Sloan, Jr., former chairman of the Board of Directors of General Motors. He stated that since the early 1920s "the basic elements of financial control in General Motors are cost, price, volume, and rate of return on investment."[34] These items, as is well known, depend upon accurate and timely profit and loss data.

The next evidence submitted in support of the aforementioned conclusions is a comparative internal income statement (Illustration VI) and a comparative external earnings statement (Illustration VII) for 1907 of the American Telephone & Telegraph Company. These two illustrations also indicate the greater detail accorded items in the internal income statement. For example, expenses were listed separately for internal purposes, whereas only one figure was presented in the external statement.

The final evidential support consisted of an interview with W.

---

[34] Alfred P. Sloan, Jr., *My Years with General Motors,* p. 140.

ILLUSTRATION VI

AMERICAN TELEPHONE & TELEGRAPH COMPANY
COMBINED EARNINGS AND EXPENSES OF ALL BELL OPERATING
COMPANIES IN THE UNITED STATES INCLUDING AT&T
(INSTRUMENT RENTAL AND OTHER DUPLICATIONS EXCLUDED)

Gross Earnings	1906	1907	Increase
Exchange service	xxxx	xxxx	xxxx
Toll service	xxxx	xxxx	xxxx
Total telephone earnings	xxxx	xxxx	xxxx
Private line service	xxxx	xxxx	xxxx
Sub-licensee service	xxxx	xxxx	xxxx
Messenger	xxxx	xxxx	xxxx
Real estate	xxxx	xxxx	xxxx
Dividends and interest	xxxx	xxxx	xxxx
Miscellaneous	xxxx	xxxx	xxxx
Total other earnings	xxxx	xxxx	xxxx
Total gross earnings	xxxx	xxxx	xxxx

Expenses

	1906	1907	Increase
General	xxxx	xxxx	xxxx
Operating	xxxx	xxxx	xxxx
Maintenance	xxxx	xxxx	xxxx
Total telephone expenses	xxxx	xxxx	xxxx
Private line	xxxx	xxxx	xxxx
Sub-license	xxxx	xxxx	xxxx
Messenger	xxxx	xxxx	xxxx
Real estate	xxxx	xxxx	xxxx
Miscellaneous	xxxx	xxxx	xxxx
Total other expenses	xxxx	xxxx	xxxx
Total expenses (except interest)	xxxx	xxxx	xxxx

Net Earnings

	1906	1907	Increase
Deduct interest balance	xxxx	xxxx	xxxx
	xxxx	xxxx	xxxx
Dividends declared by licensee companies	xxxx	xxxx	xxxx
By AT&T	xxxx	xxxx	xxxx

ILLUSTRATION VI (continued)

Total dividends	xxxx	xxxx	xxxx
Deduct dividends received			
by AT&T from licensee companies	xxxx	xxxx	xxxx
Dividends (duplications excluded)	xxxx	xxxx	xxxx
Undivided profits	xxxx	xxxx	xxxx

ILLUSTRATION VII

AMERICAN TELEPHONE & TELEGRAPH COMPANY
COMPARATIVE STATEMENT OF EARNINGS AND EXPENSES

	1906	1907
Earnings:		
Dividends	xxxx	xxxx
Interest and other revenue		
from associated and licensed companies	xxxx	xxxx
Telephone traffic (net)	xxxx	xxxx
Real estate	xxxx	xxxx
Other sources	xxxx	xxxx
Expenses	xxxx	xxxx
Net Earnings	xxxx	xxxx
Deduct interest	xxxx	xxxx
Dividends paid	xxxx	xxxx
Balance	xxxx	xxxx
Carried to reserves	xxxx	xxxx
Carried to surplus	xxxx	xxxx

Dean Reed, assistant comptroller of Owens-Illinois Corporation. During the course of the interview, selected internal income statements from 1907, the beginning of the company, until the 1940 period were reviewed. The format of the income statement did not change appreciably during the period examined, except to accommodate the changing scope of operations. If anything, the complexity of these early statements was reduced between 1907 and 1940. This reduction was the result of two forces. First, as more modern technology was applied to accounting methods and procedures the centralization of accounting functions became possible. For example, the accounts receivable, accounts payable, and payroll records were consolidated and no longer a task for individual plants. Second, the reorganization of the company into separate operating divisions, along with the development of cost centers and responsibility accounting, resulted in a reduction in the complexity of company and plant-wide internal income statements even though the complexity and frequency of lower level supporting reports were increased.

The significant point, as the above evidence reveals, is that there was no shift in emphasis from the balance sheet to the income statement as the primary accounting report for managerial use. The latter report, according to Reed, was always the prime report throughout his company's history.

SUMMARY

This chapter discussed the new emphasis on profit and loss data by internal management of a firm that generally appeared between 1885 and 1930. A long chain of ideas and events were presented that eventually culminated with income data being considered of utmost importance to a successful evaluation of a company's operations as a guide to future action.

The beginning force that set this chain of ideas and events into motion was the numerous inventions that appeared in England shortly after 1750, even though they were themselves the result of many complex and remote causes. These inventions helped pave the way for the industrialization of society through the use of the factory system. Even though old forms of business organization, particularly the sole proprietorship, still dominated at the outset, the increasing need for huge amounts of capital was soon felt. This need was accentuated by a series of inventions around 1860: (1) the Bessemer process, (2) the perfection of the dynamo, and (3) the internal combustion engine.

The original reaction to these new inventions and economic circumstances was the emergence of what has been called industrial capitalism, based on the partnership or joint-stock company form of business organization. The industrial capitalist despised financial statements; yet his tactics of cutthroat competition and emphasis on efficiency created an industrial community where investment requirements were tremendous and survival very tenuous. Thus, conditions were ripe for a type of business organization that could provide the necessary capital and yet reduce the high degree of personal liability. As a result, the corporate form of business organization, through the help of the so-called financial capitalist, became popular.

The financial capitalists tended to spread their interests over many businesses and were instrumental in many reorganizations and consolidations. As a result, managers were appointed to assume the function of operating the business. A new managerial class developed which found it necessary to use accounting and related statistics in its decisions since no one individual possessed the breadth of knowledge or the time or energy to make all the decisions. Income and expense data for the purpose of testing the profitability of operations as a guide to future action became an integral part of the accounting data required by these professional managers. On the other hand, balance sheet data were considered the more important to the financial capitalist and other external parties.

The last topic presented as evidence of this internal shift in emphasis was reference to the works of the cost accountants and scientific management writers. Furthermore, reference was made to certain replies from various corporations which indicated that income and expense data were highly significant for internal purposes long before the external shift in emphasis occurred in the early 1930s.

3

The External Shift from Balance Sheet to Income Statement

It was suggested in chapter two that developments in British and American law and auditing were the major factors in preserving the balance sheet in a position of prominence over the income statement as the primary external financial report until well into the 1930s. For example, the Joint Stock Companies Act of 1844 in Britain required the presentation of a "full and fair" balance sheet to the stockholders but did not even suggest that an income statement be presented. Furthermore, it was also stated that this policy was continued in Section 94 of the 1862 act when it stated that the auditors must disclose "whether in their opinion the balance sheet is a full and fair balance sheet."

Although similar legislation in the United States did not appear, the rise of financial capitalism and the emergence of the so-called balance sheet audit produced the same effect. This prominence, however, did not last. The income statement eventually superseded the balance sheet in terms of importance to external parties. By 1934 the impact of this changing emphasis was found in publications of the American Institute of Accountants. For example, its 1934 statement, "Audit of Corporate Accounts," stated:

The earning capacity is the fact of crucial importance in the valuation of an industrial enterprise, and therefore the income account is usually far more important than the balance sheet.[1]

---

[1] American Institute of Accountants, *Audit of Corporate Accounts*, p. 10.

Furthermore, by 1940 the shift to the income statement was almost entirely complete in the minds of external parties such as stockholders and creditors. George O. May stressed this fact when he wrote in the May 1937 issue of the *Journal of Accountancy* that the determination of income "is now generally recognized as the most important problem in the field of financial accounting."[2]

DOCUMENTATION OF THE EXTERNAL SHIFT

In Accounting Textbooks

In 1908 Charles E. Sprague wrote: "The balance sheet may be considered the groundwork of all accountancy, the origin and terminus of every account."[3] Likewise, Henry Rand Hatfield in his book *Modern Accounting* (1909) contended that the balance sheet was the goal of all accounting.[4] Roy B. Kester in *Accounting Theory and Practice* also maintained a similar belief.[5]

As time passed these authors tended to alter their views with respect to the importance of the balance sheet. For example, in commenting on the changes in the field of accounting since his 1909 publication, Hatfield said:

Accounting is essentially of a twofold character. It seeks to disclose the facts regarding the amount and kind of assets and liabilities. In addition to this and of equal if not superior importance, is the information which it gives in regard to the proprietorship, and the various causes which have contributed to this result. The showing of assets is the main function of the balance sheet .... The exhibit of the changes in proprietorship is embodied in an income or profit and loss statement. Each of these statements has its own value and use.[6]

Kester in the 1922 revision of *Accounting Theory and Practice* essentially upheld the importance of the balance sheet as the most useful statement, particularly for credit purposes. But in the third revised edition in 1930 he wrote:

---

[2] George O. May, "Improvements in Financial Accounts," p. 346.
[3] Charles E. Sprague, *The Philosophy of Accounts*, p. 26.
[4] Henry Rand Hatfield, *Modern Accounting*, pp. 3-4.
[5] Roy B. Kester, *Accounting Theory and Practice*, chapter one.
[6] Henry Rand Hatfield, *Accounting: Its Principles and Problems*, p. 240.

The two basic problems of accounting are concerned with the determination of: (1) the worth or proprietorship of a business at a given time; and (2) the success or failure of a business endeavor during a given or definite period of time.[7]

Kester then explained in detail that profit is a part of proprietorship in the accounting equation of asset — liabilities = proprietorship. In addition he emphasized the balance sheet approach for the calculation of income even though it is to management's advantage "to maintain the proper relationship between income and expense," implying the matching process.[8]

The fourth revised edition of 1939 has some notable changes that indicate how Kester viewed the changing emphasis from the balance sheet to the income statement. These changes were criticisms of current balance sheet constructions and the use of a new profit equation to introduce the matching concept of income — costs = profit.[9] The criticisms of the balance sheet related to the problem of datum content and value content necessary for a "clear" financial condition.[10]

Other less theoretical textbooks also indicate the shift in emphasis that occurred. In a principles text written by J. D. McKinsey, later by McKinsey and H. S. Noble, subsequently by Noble, then Noble and Niswonger, and currently by C. Rollin Niswonger and Phillip E. Fess, this change is also reflected. The first edition of 1929 considered the balance sheet as "one of the most important statements that the proprietor receives."[11] This statement was repeated in the 1935 edition [12] and the 1939 edition,[13] but it was omitted in the fourth edition in describing the importance of the balance sheet. Instead, the essence of this quoted statement was ascribed to the income statement as follows: "The amount of profit or loss incurred during a given period is the most important single fact of the period."[14] In addition, the

---

[7] Roy B. Kester, *Accounting Theory and Practice* (1930 edition, vol. 1), p. 35.

[8] Ibid., p. 39.

[9] Ibid., 1939 edition, p. 36.

[10] Ibid., pp. 26-27.

[11] James O. McKinsey, *Accounting Principles*, p. 21.

[12] James O. McKinsey and Howard S. Noble, *Accounting Principles*, 2d. ed., p. 15.

[13] Ibid., 1939 edition, p. 7.

[14] Howard S. Noble, *Accounting Principles*, 4th ed., p. 41.

transactions approach, rather than the capital maintenance approach, to income determination was emphasized for the first time.

Robert H. Montgomery, although the champion of the balance sheet audit for many years, also reflected the increased importance of the income statement in the later editions of his book, *Auditing Theory and Practice.* For example, in the first edition of 1912 he stated that "where there is an audit department properly conducted, or where the purpose of the examination is to determine the net worth of the concern, the auditor will usually confine himself entirely to the items of the balance sheet."[15] This view continued even in his 1934 edition as others were recommending the use of the term "financial statements" and emphasizing the importance of the income statement. The following quotation indicates this view:

> The importance of the balance sheet not only as the ultimate goal in the conduct of an audit but also as a basis for the determination of audit procedure, warrants attention.[16]

Furthermore, the income account was still being treated as a supplement to the balance sheet, although he admits that an audit is not completed until it also is examined.[17]

The 1940 sixth revision contained some changes over the earlier editions, reflecting among other things the change in emphasis from the balance sheet to the income statement, the pronouncements of the American Institute of Accountants, the American Accounting Association, and the SEC. Most notable was the use of the term financial statements in reference to the extent of the audit and the introduction of the short form audit report. But Montgomery still has a yearning for the "old" balance sheet prominence as is evidenced by the following passage:

> In recent years great stress has been laid on the importance of the income statement to an understanding by investors and others of the financial affairs of a corporation. It is said that the value of a business, and consequently of its assets, depends almost entirely on its earning power. Because of this feeling, there has been a tendency to belittle the balance sheet as a source of information, and to view the accounting problems largely from the

---

[15] Robert H. Montgomery, *Auditing Theory and Practice,* p. 72.
[16] Ibid., 1934 edition, p. 78.
[17] Ibid., p. 456.

point of view of the income statement ... however, the balance sheet also has information for the intelligent reader which, in some circumstances at least, is of equal importance to that displayed in the income statement.[18]

Many other works could be cited as evidence of the shift from the balance sheet to the income statement. But the point is clear that the groundwork for the shift was laid in the 1920s, accentuated in the 1930s, and completed by 1940.

IN FINANCIAL REPORTS OF CORPORATIONS

A brief survey of some of the older published annual reports, shown in Illustration VIII reveals that there was a gradual emergence, not a

ILLUSTRATION VIII

LIST OF ANNUAL REPORTS REVIEWED

Company	Reports Reviewed
1. Allis-Chalmers Company	1912-15; 1917-50
2. American Can Company	1915-50
3. Anaconda Company	1915-50
4. B. F. Goodrich Company	1914-50
5. E. I. du Pont deNémours and Company	1914-50
6. F. W. Woolworth Company	1914-50
7. General Electric Company	1893-1950
8. General Motors Company	1916-50
9. International Harvester Company	1917-50
10. Owens-Illinois	1907-50
11. P. Lorillard Company	1924-50
12. Procter & Gamble Company	1919-50
13. Pullman Incorporated	1920-50
14. Republic Steel Company	1918-50
15. Sears, Roebuck & Company	1906-50
16. Standard Oil Company of New Jersey	1918-50
17. U.S. Rubber Company (Uniroyal)	1892-1950
18. United Fruit Company	1900-50
19. United States Steel Corporation	1912-50
20. Westinghouse Electric	1906-50

---

[18] Ibid., 1940 edition, p. 59.

sudden or dramatic appearance, of the presentation of income statement data as they are reported today. Furthermore, it seemed apparent that there was no significant decline in the complexity of the balance sheet. In fact, the contrary was observed, that is, balance sheets became more and more complete and informative in terms of today's standards. But the important point is that income information in early reports either was nonexistent or consisted of a simple T account copied from the ledger, whereas, the balance sheet was the main center of attraction. This situation changed over the years until, by 1950, eighteen of the twenty companies examined displayed modern type income statements. Thus, it might be said that there was actually no shift in emphasis but simply the emergence of income reporting from either no data at all or rudimentary presentations to the income statement as it is known today. This emergence, although starting in the 1920s and early 1930s, was accelerated after the creation of the SEC and was essentially completed by the mid-1940s as the following examples will show.

In its third annual report of 1895 General Electric presented a consolidated profit and loss account as shown in Illustration IX. Yet despite this inclusion, the report highlighted a discussion of the valuation of assets, reassuring the stockholders that all assets were conservatively valued. In 1912 the company published a crude "condensed profit and loss account" in multiple-step form. Even though this was an advancement, in terms of today's standards of presentation, the report still highlighted balance sheet data. In its 1926 annual report, a comparative statement of income and expenses replaced the old condensed profit and loss account as shown in Illustration X. Yet, little explanatory information was provided for income statement items. It was not until the 1930 annual report that the company presented detailed data as to earnings both past and present. By 1941 the emergence of income reporting was essentially completed for the General Electric Company. The annual report for that year contained detailed explanations of each section of the income statement, including appropriate explanations of tax expense, depreciation, and even dividends. In fact, at the beginning of the report there was a special section entitled highlights of the year containing sales, profits, dividends, and earnings per share data.

In its first annual report of 1893 the United States Rubber Company (Uniroyal) included a balance sheet in modern type report format, but included no income statement data or sales data. The tenth annual report of 1903 included a crude consolidated income statement as

ILLUSTRATION IX

GENERAL ELECTRIC

CONSOLIDATED PROFIT AND LOSS ACCOUNT OF JANUARY 31, 1895

Adjusted balance as of January 31, 1894		xxxx	Business of the Current Year:	
Business of the Current Year:			Sales	xxxx
Cost of goods sold	xxxx		Royalties and sundry profits	xx	xxxx
Legal and general expenses and taxes	xxxx	xxxx	Interest and dividends on		
Interest on Debentures	xxxx	xxxx	securities owned	xxxx	
Losses Chargeable Partly to Previous			Interest and discount	xxxx	xxxx
and Partly to Current Years' Business:				
Consignments and contracts written				
off		xxxx		
Additional depreciation allowed for:				
On plants, consignments, and				
contracts	xxxx			
On notes and accounts				
receivable	xxxx	xxxx xxxx		
Further Amounts Now Charged Off:				
Patents and franchises	xxxx			
Various inventories	xxxx			
Sundry losses	xxxx	xxxx xxxx	Balance, January 31, 1895	xxxx xxxx

ILLUSTRATION X

GENERAL ELECTRIC COMPANY
COMPARATIVE STATEMENT OF INCOME AND EXPENSES

	1926	1925
Net sales billed	xxxx	xxxx
Less: cost of sales billed, including operating, maintenance and depreciation charges, reserves, and provision for all taxes	xxxx	xxxx
Net income from sales	xxxx	xxxx
Income from other sources:		
Income from associated companies	xxxx	xxxx
Income from miscellaneous securities	xxxx	xxxx
Interest and discount	xxxx	xxxx
Income from U.S. government securities	xxxx	xxxx
Royalties and sundry revenue	xxxx	xxxx
	xxxx	xxxx
Total income	xxxx	xxxx
Less: all interest payments and in 1925, premium on debentures retired	xxxx	xxxx
Addition to general reserve	xxxx	xxxx
	xxxx	xxxx
Profit available for dividends	xxxx	xxxx
Less: 6 percent cash dividends on special stock	xxxx	xxxx
Profit available for dividends on special stock	xxxx	xxxx
Less: cash dividends on common stock	xxxx	xxxx
Surplus for the year	xxxx	xxxx
Surplus at January 1	xxxx	xxxx
	xxxx	xxxx
Less: dividends paid in special stock:	xxxx	xxxx
$1 per share in 1926 (equivalent to $4 per share on old $100 par value stock) and $5 per share in 1925	xxxx	xxxx
Surplus at December 31	xxxx	xxxx

shown in Illustration XI. The detail and information contained in this first statement left something to be desired. Although the income statement changed gradually over the next fifteen years, it was the 1928 annual report that evoked comments by the auditors in their opinion letter and the chairman in his letter to the stockholders as to the need for more elaborate figures in the income statement. By the

ILLUSTRATION XI

U.S. RUBBER COMPANY
AND SUBSIDIARY COMPANIES
CONSOLIDATED INCOME STATEMENT FOR YEAR ENDING MARCH 31, 1903

Gross sales, boots and shoes	xxxx
Net sales, boots, shoes, and miscellaneous	xxxx
Cost of goods sold	xxxx
Manufacturing profits	xxxx
Freight, taxes, insurance, general and selling expenses	xxxx
Operating profits	xxxx
Other income	xxxx
Total income	xxxx
Less:	
Interest and commissions on funding	
Notes and borrowed money	xxxx
Interest on Boston Rubber Shoe Company	
Debentures	xxxx
Interest allowed customers for prepayments	xxxx
Net income to surplus	xxxx
Deductions from surplus and bad debts	xxxx
Surplus for period	xxxx
April 1, 1902	xxxx
March 31, 1903	xxxx

1936 annual report there was increased attention given to profit and loss figures. In addition, the income statement, for the first time, was presented in comparative form as shown in Illustration XII. Finally, by 1942 the annual report contained detailed explanations of the items included in the income statement. In short, the emergence of income reporting for Uniroyal was also essentially completed.

General Motors and particularly United States Steel Corporation are good examples of the early development of income reporting. Other companies, however, did not develop modern type income reporting until well into the 1930s and sometimes the early 1940s, even though most published rather comprehensive balance sheets much earlier.

Standard Oil Company of New Jersey published a verbose, but quantitatively lacking, report in 1918. It was not until a "revision in

ILLUSTRATION XII

U.S. RUBBER COMPANY AND SUBSIDIARY COMPANIES
CONSOLIDATED INCOME

	1936	1935
Sales, after all returns, discounts, excise and sales taxes, transportation, and allowances	xxxx	xxxx
Cost of goods sold, including depreciation of $5,535,346 for 1936 and $5,581,878 for 1935	xxxx	xxxx
Gross profit	xxxx	xxxx
Administrative and general expenses	xxxx	xxxx
Profit from operations	xxxx	xxxx
Dividends received from affiliated companies in 1936; from U.S. Rubber Plantations, Inc. in 1935	xxxx	xxxx
Deferred income credits, less charges	xxxx	xxxx
	xxxx	xxxx
Interest on funded indebtedness	xxxx	xxxx
Net income before provisions	xxxx	xxxx
Provision for federal income taxes ($2,371,206 for 1936; $1,488,441 for 1935), undistributed profits tax of subsidiaries ($874 for 1936; none for 1935) and foreign income taxes	xxxx	xxxx
Provision for fluctuation in raw material prices	xxxx	xxxx
Net income for the period	xxxx	xxxx

the chart of accounts and accounting procedure, in conformity with accepted principles of accounting, which became effective on January 1, 1934"[19] that a modern type consolidated income statement was published. Sears, Roebuck & Company in its 1908 annual report also presented figures for gross sales, sales returns and allowances, dividends, and selling expenses along with a rather elaborate balance sheet in modern report form. But it was not until 1920 that a simple income statement was published and 1930 for the first comparative income statement. In 1935 the annual report contained the first income statement as it is presented today by the company. By 1941 bold

---

[19] Report of the *Standard Oil Company* (incorporated in New Jersey), for the year ended December 31, 1934, p. 13.

captions reported the financial highlights, particularly earnings per share, net sales, and dividends, among others.

Other examples could be presented; but the results would be similar. In particular, the emergence of income reporting was a phenomenon of the 1930s and early 1940s even though earlier examples can be found.

IN *Journal of Accountancy* EDITORIALS

Reference should be made to the changing emphasis as reflected in editorial releases of the *Journal of Accountancy,* since this publication more than any other is representative of the state of "actual" accounting theory and practice.

Until 1928 editorials in the *Journal* were specifically geared to emphasizing the significance of the balance sheet; however, in the February issue of that year A. P. Richardson, editor, commented on the importance of Irving Fisher's definition of income to accounting.[20] In December of the same year there was an editorial denying the fact that the balance sheet reflects "future earning power" as some had advocated.[21]

In the January 1929 issue the editor suggested that the need for an accepted definition of net profits was an "illustration of the imperative need for agreement upon the meaning of phrases so that they may be something more than 'just words.' "[22] This reflected the increased concern with income calculations. The May 1930 editorial contained a discussion of the importance of earnings per share that had attracted a good deal of attention at that time. The editorial stated that "we do not believe that the earnings 'per share' play as an important a part in the creation of market values as a good many people seem to think."[23]

The first editorial to specifically mention the reporting problems created by the enormous increase in the number of shareholders in corporations in the past fifteen years was in the July 1930 issue. Here the editor stated that "the enormous increase which has taken place in the number of shareholders in corporations in the past fifteen

---

[20] Editorial, "Income Defined at Last," pp. 125-27.
[21] Editorial, "The Meaning of a Balance Sheet," pp. 445-46.
[22] Editorial, "What Are Net Profits?" pp. 44-46.
[23] Editorial, "Earning Per Share," p. 323.

years has attracted the attention of the public to the financial statements of corporations whose stocks are bought and sold for the purposes of investment and speculation."[24] But it was not until the June
1932 issue that the question of income was discussed at any length.[25]
In the March 1934 issue the shift to emphasis on the problems resulting from the calculation of income in editorial presentations was
essentially completed.[26] It was in this issue that a review appeared of
the American Institute of Accountant's publication, *Audit of Corporate Accounts.* This document, as has been mentioned before, contended that the income account is in most instances more important
than the balance sheet. The editorial policy also clearly began to
reflect this fact.

In Memorandums on Balance Sheet Audits

The 1917 memorandum, *Approved Methods for the Preparation of
Balance-Sheet Statements,* prepared by the American Institute of Accountants at the request of the Federal Trade Commission, indicated
the emphasis on providing information for creditors through the
balance sheet. In 1929, another edition, *Verification of Financial
Statements (Revised),* was published. This revision, like the earlier
edition, set forth suggestions for the verification and preparation of
statements, particularly the balance sheet. But the emphasis on certain
profit and loss statement items, such as depreciation, indicated the
increasing attention devoted to income data.

As far as the balance sheet was concerned, most instructions related
to the audit and presentation of balance sheet accounts while advocating the use of the cost or market, whichever is lower, rule. On
the other hand, departures from the cost basis of accounting were
allowed "if the property valuation is stated on the basis of an appraisal at a given date."[27]

The 1936 revision, *Examination of Financial Statements by Independent Public Accountants,* serves as additional evidence of the external shift in emphasis to the income statement over the 1929 edition. For example, the preface states:

---

[24] Editorial, "Clear Statements Needed," pp. 5-6.
[25] Editorial, "What Is Income?" pp. 401-2.
[26] Editorial, *Journal of Accountancy,* March 1934, pp. 168-72.
[27] U. S. Government, *Verification of Financial Statements (Revised),* p. 13.

Development of accounting practice during recent years has been in the direction of increased emphasis on accounting principles and consistency in their application.... The suggestions contained in this bulletin are intended to apply to examinations by independent public accountants of financial statements prepared for credit purposes or for *Annual reports to stockholders.*[28]

The following quotations from the 1936 revision indicate the changing external shift in emphasis from the balance sheet to the income statement for investors and other external parties:

1. From an investor's point of view, it is generally recognized today that earning capacity is of vital importance and that the *income account is at least as important as the balance sheet.*[29]

2. The development of accounting conventions has been influenced largely by a recognition of the importance of the income account. As a rule, the first objective has been to secure a proper charge or credit to the income account for the year, and in general the presumption has been that once this is achieved, the residual amount of the expenditure or the receipt can properly find its place in the balance sheet at the close of the period. Thus the changes in the balance sheet from year to year are in many aspects *more significant* than the balance sheets themselves.[30]

One of the important features of the 1936 bulletin was the absence of all mention of the balance sheet audit. Instead, the use of the term "examination of financial statements" was substituted. Thus, one of the main factors temporarily counteracting those forces which normally would have shifted the emphasis from the balance sheet to the income statement earlier had been eliminated.

FACTORS AFFECTING THE EXTERNAL SHIFT

The rise of the corporation with the separation of owners and managers was a prime factor in the growing emphasis on income statement data. This was in contrast to earlier periods where the major function of accounting statements was to provide information for credit purposes. Creditors were mostly interested in the financial posi-

---

[28] American Institute of Accountants, *Examination of Financial Statements by Independent Public Accountants,* p. v. (Italics added for emphasis.)

[29] Ibid., p. 4. (Italics added for emphasis.)

[30] Ibid., pp. 4-5. (Italics added for emphasis.)

tion of a borrower. The balance sheet seemed sufficient to fulfill this need. Furthermore, its content had been designed with this need in mind. William A. Paton reflected this point of view when he wrote:

The periodic statement of assets and equities, if well arranged, throws much light upon the position of the several interests from the standpoint of safety of principle . . . . With respect to a single balance sheet this is especially true in the case of short term creditors. The bank which is extending a sixty-day loan to an enterprise, for example, is interested above all in the probable cash position of the concern at the date of payment, and the comparison of liquid assets and current liabilities which is facilitated by the balance sheet is highly significant in this connection.[31]

The growing widespread ownership of stock that began early in this century and accelerated rapidly in the 1920s tended to shift the spotlight from creditors, such as banks, to the providers of equity capital. This latter group was not only interested in the amount of their investment, but also in the factors contributing to its growth or lack of growth. Stephen Gilman made this point clear in his 1939 book:

While the creditor's rights are still considered of great importance, the stockholder, who was previously the forgotten man of finance, has found champions who insist that accounting owes an obligation not only to him who supplies temporary capital but also to him who supplies permanent capital.[32]

The stockholders as a group were primarily interested in the prospective return on their investment through dividends and the growth in the price of their shares. In addition, since they were removed from the day-to-day operations of the business, there was a tendency to seek useful, readily-understood information on the efficiency of management. A single gauge of value, if developed, would certainly be a tremendous aid to the relatively uneducated and bewildered investor who was looking for a simple way of ascertaining where to invest funds.

Accounting responded to this new demand by placing greater emphasis upon the income statement. But this new emphasis did not appear overnight. It took the interaction of ideas and events before the increased emphasis occurred. Of all the important ideas, one of the most influential consisted of the popularization of the entity theory

---

[31] William A. Paton, *Accounting*, p. 479.
[32] Stephen Gilman, *Accounting Concepts of Profit*, pp. 27-28

and the going-concern assumption by Paton. Paton noted this when he wrote in 1940:

Another important result of using the enterprise as the focus of attention has been the development of the going-concern assumption, with derivative stressing of the interpretation of business operation as a continuing stream of activity. The increasing consideration being given to income measurement and reporting is presumably a manifestation of the influence of the business-enterprise managerial point of view.[33]

Many events were important factors in the new emphasis on profits. There are three, however, that were more important than any others—the awakened interest in the investor's viewpoint, the fluctuations in the prices of goods and services that began in the early 1920s, and the influence of government taxation and legislation.

THE ENTITY THEORY AND GOING-CONCERN POSTULATE

The emergence of the entity theory and the corollary concept of the going-concern in response to the rise of the corporate form of organization interacted with the economist's concept of profit as surplus entrepreneurial remuneration to provide the theoretical groundwork for the shift in emphasis from the balance sheet to the income statement in financial accounting.

Although development of the entity theory during the latter part of the nineteenth century occurred in Germany, Paton was primarily responsible for its introduction and expansion in the United States. In the 1922 edition of *Accounting Theory,* he clearly recognized "the relations between certain accounting concepts and fundamental classes of economic theory."[34] For example, in discussing one of his fundamental classes "properties," he wrote:

A consideration of the relation of the class, "properties," to the economist's concept, "wealth," will serve to throw some light upon the fundamental nature of this accounting category. In general it may be said that anything which can constitute wealth may, under certain circumstances, become an asset to the accountant.[35]

---

[33] William A. Paton, "Recent and Prospective Developments in Accounting Theory," in *Selected Readings in Accounting and Auditing,* p. 28.
[34] William A. Paton, *Accounting Theory,* p. v.
[35] Ibid., p. 33.

Furthermore, he stated: "Evidently the accountant's class, properties, is somewhat akin to the economist's capital."[36]

The most significant relation between economics and accounting for the purposes of this study was his adoption of the entity theory. In the preface of *Accounting Theory* he wrote:

In this book ... an attempt has been made to present a restatement of the theory of accounting consistent with the conditions and needs of the business enterprise "par excellence," the large corporation, as well as applicable to the simpler, more primitive forms of organization. The conception of the business enterprise as in all cases a distinct entity or personality—an extension of the fiction of the corporate entity—is adopted ....[37]

Further, on the postulates of accounting Paton stated:

The concept of the business entity is constantly used outside the corporate form of organization by economists and others interested in the business process.[38]

Along with the entity theory the concept of "going concern" was also listed as a corollary postulate. Littleton contended that the "relationship between regular periodic reporting and the concept of enterprise continuity is clearly evident." Particularly, he believed that "periodic reports were the consequence of the acceptance of the idea of enterprise continuity."[39] With the acceptance of the entity theory and periodic reporting, the groundwork in theory was complete for the shift in emphasis from the balance sheet to the income statement and the development of the transactions approach to income accounting. To use Emily Chen Chang's words:

The income statement is elevated as the most significant financial statement, an exhibition of management accomplishments and a measurement of the corporation's earning power; while the balance sheet is belittled as a means of carrying forward unamortized acquisition prices, an exhibition of unfinished jobs. The business entity is the center of attention, and the interests of individual stockholders are pushed into the background.[40]

---

[36] Ibid., p. 35.

[37] Ibid., p. v.

[38] Ibid., p. 373.

[39] A. C. Littleton and V. K. Zimmerman, *Accounting Theory: Continuity and Change,* pp. 55-56.

[40] Emily Chen Chang, "Business Income in Accounting and Economics," *Accounting Review,* October 1962, p. 638.

THE CHANGING PRICE LEVEL

Before the 1930s historical costs emerged as the "generally accepted" basis for reflecting balance sheet values only because it was generally thought that these historical cost figures approximated value. In short, although historical cost figures were accepted, firms did not hesitate to write assets up or down because the balance sheet tended to be treated as a statement of valuations. This view was expressed by many early writers particularly in their treatment of depreciation as essentially a valuation concept.[41] As a result, "among the many kinds of financial statements which confront the man in business today, the balance sheet holds the most important place."[42]

The march of events, the sharp decline in prices in 1921-1923, prompted many individuals to start questioning the utility of the balance sheet. For example, Littleton contended in 1923 that the fluctuating price level renders the customary balance sheet ineffective at times as a guide to action. Nevertheless, he contended that cost should be consistently used in all accounts and statements.[43] Eric Kohler in a 1936 issue of the *Accounting Review* also argued that balance sheets are misleading and are actually a liability to the financial analysts. Furthermore, he contended that balance sheets are less than satisfactory because a common valuation basis for each of the terms is lacking.[44]

The initial reaction to these attacks on the balance sheet was to focus attention on principles of valuation in an effort to improve the stature of the report. Although the literature on this subject is quite extensive, the most outstanding contribution was by an economist, John B. Canning. In his book, *The Economics of Accountancy*, he stated, "an attempt will be made to describe their (accountants) valuation process and to suggest certain means whereby this process may, in due course, be changed for the better."[45]

Another group of accountants led by Littleton, Paton, and others

---

[41] See for example William Morse Cole, *Accounts, Their Construction and Interpretation*, pp. 70-80, and Earl Saliers, *Principles of Depreciation*, pp. 139-73.

[42] Chester B. Couchman, *The Balance Sheet*, p. 3.

[43] A. C. Littleton, "Principles of Valuation as Related to the Balance Sheet," pp. 14-15.

[44] Eric L. Kohler, "Tendencies in Balance Sheet Construction," pp. 1-3.

[45] John B. Canning, *The Economics of Accountancy*, p. 198.

responded to these fluctuating prices by advocating strict adherence to historical costs because value is subjective instead of changing valuation bases. Littleton pointed out this dilemma between those who believe balance sheets should represent "value" and those, like himself, who ascribed to the cost principle as follows:

Balance sheets by valuation . . . create serious problems of income determination. . . . Yet, on the other hand, neither is accountancy able to hold to the purely cost, or outlay, balance sheets, because to do so, it is thought, would destroy the instrument as "a statement of values" which seems to be the *sine qua non* of credit granting.[46]

He then argued that cost prices are recorded in accounting because they are ascertainable facts, not because they represent value. If accountants were to keep supplying accurate financial data then they must stay with cost prices and not "venture outside the realm of known facts" where value is found.[47]

The collapse of the stock market in the autumn of 1929 and the Great Depression that followed naturally led to a loss of confidence in the balance sheet and a desire for something new and more reliable for the purpose of analyzing investment alternatives. The speculative orgy of the pre-depression days based on frequent and optimistic revaluations of assets, dividend distributions based on inflated values, and heavy reliance on book value of stock had ended.[48] Prices, wages, interest, rents, and profits decreased drastically in the early years of the 1930s. Assets were no longer the most important element in success—it was income.

In conjunction with the Great Depression and the legislation that it triggered, the national departure from the gold standard was the final blow to the question of asset valuation. It was felt that accounts must now reflect dates of acquisition because dollars changed value. Otherwise, no additivity of asset values would be possible. An editorial in the *Journal of Accountancy* made this point clear:

Its [departure from gold standard] complications are almost limitless, and if the accountant is to be absolutely logical he will probably find himself confronted with the necessity of building up a scheme of dating . . . .[49]

---

[46] A. C. Littleton, "Value and Price in Accounting," p. 148.
[47] Ibid., p. 153.
[48] John Kenneth Galbraith, *The Great Crash,* p. 174.
[49] Editorial, "Fruits of Experiment," p. 321.

EMERGENCE OF THE INVESTORS' VIEWPOINT

As was mentioned before, the rapid growth of stock ownership by the general public after World War I began to create a new demand for information. Three men, William Z. Ripley, J. M. B. Hoxsey, and George O. May were no doubt the best exponents of this emerging point of view. Ripley stated his case for an improvement in accounting standards for annual reporting as early as 1915 when he criticized the accounting practices of railroads.[50] But it was in his 1927 book, *Main Street and Wall Street,* portions of which had appeared as articles, that he attacked the accounting information available to stockholders and investors. In *Main Street and Wall Street,* which are synonyms for the phenomena of widespread ownership and the financial power in our great capital centers respectively, he stated that "the sudden advent of widespread popular ownership of corporations since the World War had created entirely new circumstances and conditions in the business world."[51] As a result of these new circumstances he argued that two essentials were needed to provide better accounting data: "an adequate balance sheet and income statement."[52] Of the two, the income statement "is perhaps more significant both immediately and prophetically." Yet, of the two, "it is the income statement that is more apt to be suppressed."[53] He then made a scathing attack on the state of current annual reporting by stating, for example, that "Singer Manufacturing Company produced a 'picture-book' annual report" whereas, "National Biscuit Company doesn't include such 'newfangled gewgaws as income accounts or depreciation.' "[54]

J. M. B. Hoxsey, as executive assistant to the Committee on Stock List of the New York Stock Exchange, addressed the annual convention of the American Institute of Accountants in 1930. In this address he pointed out:

The need of accurate information for the aid of management is still paramount; but, under conditions of today, the next object in order of importance has become to give to stockholders, in understandable form, such informa-

---

[50] William Z. Ripley, *Railroads, Finance and Organization.*
[51] William Z. Ripley, *Main Street and Wall Street,* p. 156.
[52] Ibid., p. 171.
[53] Ibid., p. 172.
[54] Ibid., p. 162.

tion in regard to the business as will avoid misleading them in any respect and as well put them in possession of all information needed, and which can be supplied in financial statements, to determine the true value of their investment.[55]

He then made a plea that accountants should refrain from certifying financial statements unless adequate information as to interest, cumulative dividends, sinking funds, sales or gross revenue, operating and other income, and surplus are included.[56]

The New York Stock Exchange also recognized the emergence of the investor's viewpoint. As a result, in 1930 the exchange recognized the need to cooperate with the American Institute of Accountants. Thus, in 1930 the American Institute of Accountants appointed a special committee on cooperation with stock exchanges. This new committee, under the direction of George O. May, in an effort to improve the quality of financial reporting, recommended certain objectives to the New York Stock Exchange. These objectives emphasized the fact that the earning capacity of a business is of crucial significance in ascertaining the value of its assets. These recommendations as presented below will reflect this emphasis.

1. To bring about a better recognition by the investing public of the fact that the balance sheet of a large modern corporation does not and should not be expected to represent an attempt to show present values of assets and liabilities of the corporation.

2. To emphasize the fact that balance sheets are necessarily to a large extent historical and conventional in character....

3. To emphasize the cardinal importance of the income account, such importance being explained by the fact that the value of the business is dependent mainly on its earning capacity....

4. To make universal the acceptance by listed corporations of certain broad principles of accounting which have won fairly general acceptance, and within the limits of such broad principles to make no attempt to restrict the right of corporations to select detailed methods of accounting deemed by them to be best adapted to the requirement of their business....[57]

These objectives clearly indicated the importance now beginning to be accorded the income statement. These recommendations were

---

[55] J. M. B. Hoxsey, "Accounting for Investors," p. 252.
[56] Ibid., pp. 259-61.
[57] American Institute of Accountants, *Audits of Corporate Accounts*.

widely circulated and helped make corporations aware of their responsibility for financial reporting. Also, they were deemed so important that the essence of these recommendations was subsequently adopted as part of the philosophy of the SEC.

Other Factors Influencing the External Shift

Many other ideas and events contributed to the shift in emphasis from the balance sheet to the income statement. The activities of financial analysts contributed to this shift because of their criticisms and analysis of financial statements. For example, from the latter part of the nineteenth century the work of analysts, particularly in the area of ratio analysis, underwent changes that were similar to those previously mentioned in accounting. In the early period (1900-1919), ratio analysis was divided into credit analysis emphasizing the ability to pay and managerial analysis emphasizing profitability measures.[58] This situation reflected the use of the balance sheet for external parties and the income statement by management.

The decade from 1920 to 1929 resulted in increased activity by financial analysts. The writers of this period, such as James Bliss and Stephen Gilman, began to view the function of financial management as an integral part of overall management instead of a staff speciality concerned with fund raising.[59] Attempts were made to develop ratios that reflected the relationships between costs, revenues, turnover, earnings, and other fundamental relationships in an effort to find better gauges of the value of a firm's securities.[60] These relationships naturally required accurate information that should be contained in income statements. Consequently, financial analysts began to exert pressure for better income statements. Thus, they, too, were a force contributing to the shift in emphasis.

Another factor contributing to the external shift in emphasis came from the courts which advocated that accounting should reflect that income which is legally available for dividends. This legal-dividend emphasis also was incorporated into various state laws. The famous American Malting Company court case (*Hutchinson* v. *Curtiss*, 92

---

[58] James O. Horrigan, "A Short History of Financial Ratio Analysis," pp. 284-85.

[59] Ezra Solomon, *The Theory of Financial Management*, p. 2.

[60] James O. Horrigan, "Financial Ratio Aanalysis," p. 287.

N.Y.S. 70, 1904) held that contracts calling for future delivery and payments were not a basis for declaring dividends because such dividends would be mere "paper profits." In the 1885 case of *Jennery* v. *Olmstead* (36 Hun 536, affirmed 105 N.Y.S. 653, 13 N.E. 1926), it was held that appreciation in the value of United States bonds held by banks should not be taken into a profit and loss account and thus be made available for dividends. The General Corporation Law of 1927, Section 8623-28, of Ohio stated that "cash dividends shall not be paid out of surplus due to or arising from (a) unrealized appreciation in value of or revaluation of fixed assets . . . ."

The point is clear; the legal-dividend emphasis accompanying the growth of the corporation tended to result in more and more accounting questions to be answered in terms of their effect upon the income account. Thus, the income statement was considered more and more important.

Many other factors contributed to the ascendancy of the income statement—the development of national income accounting, accounting research of the American Accounting Association, the influence of regulatory commissions, the development of railroad accounting, and many others. The influence of government legislation and taxation will be presented in the next chapter.

SUMMARY

This chapter was concerned with the external shift in emphasis from the balance sheet to the income statement that began in the 1920s, accelerated in the 1930s, and culminated in the early 1940s.

A documentation of this external shift was evidenced by the transition in accounting textbooks, financial reports of corporations, the *Journal of Accountancy* editorials, and in the publications of the American Institute of Accountants.

There were many factors affecting the shift in emphasis. The rise of the corporate form of business organization in response to the industrialization of society was a prime factor in the growing emphasis on profits. This new emphasis manifested itself in an internal shift in emphasis that was discussed in chapter two. The external shift occurred after the internal shift and resulted from the interaction of ideas and events. The most influential ideas consisted of the popularization of the entity theory and the going-concern assumption by Paton, Littleton, and others.

Many events were important factors to the external shift. The most important three were: the awakened interest in the investors' viewpoint, the rapid fluctuation in the prices of goods and services that began in the early 1920s, and the influence of governmental taxation and legislation.

4

The Influence of Federal
Taxation and Legislation

The advent of income taxation and other federal legislation was a factor of marked consequence in the promotion of the income statement viewpoint. Many feel that it is not an exaggeration to say that this development has had more influence than any other factor in bringing about the ascendancy of income accounting based upon systematic accounting methods. H. C. Daines suggested:

The income tax objective is reflected in the attitude on the part of certain businessmen and accountants that the books of accounts should be kept so as to properly record the taxable income. It can be said that many believe that this point of view constitutes the primary purpose of accounting.[1]

Federal income taxation, beginning with the 1894 and 1909 acts, was firmly established with the adoption of the Sixteenth Amendment early in 1913. The passage of the first act under this amendment in 1913 and subsequent legislation imposing even higher rates based upon income and net earnings naturally led businessmen to consider it imperative that profit figures be calculated with the greatest possible degree of precision to insure that minimum legal amounts of taxes were paid. The task of computing this periodic business income was naturally the domain of the accountant. As a result, accountants

---

[1] H. C. Daines, "The Changing Objectives of Accounting," p. 103.

began to focus increased attention upon the problems associated with
the matching of costs and revenues (such as timing, recognition, allo-
cation, and so forth). The end product of this increased attention
was the tendency to present more detailed income statements, in
terms of form and content. In fact, in many cases the emergence of
income reporting for external purposes appeared in smaller companies for the first time simply because the necessary information was
prepared for tax purposes.[2] On the other hand, to suggest that the
emergence of income reporting for external parties was solely the result
of income taxation is, of course, untrue. The important point, however, is that the tax laws forced businessmen, if they wanted to mini-
mize taxes, to keep appropriate records as to revenue and expense. The
other condition that resulted in the emergence of income reporting
was, as mentioned before, the demands and legislation resulting from
the increased importance of the small investor.

FEDERAL INCOME TAXATION

THE PROBLEM OF INCOME

The taxation of income reflects the long-term shift from property to
income as a measure of economic well-being (wealth) or power.

The Sixteenth Amendment to the Constitution stated in Article
XVI:

The Congress shall have power to lay and collect taxes on incomes, from what-
ever source derived, with apportionment among the several states, and without
regard to any census or enumeration.

One of the first problems encountered as a result of this statement
was interpretation of the term income. Much confusion resulted because of the various meanings that were available. Economists, as is
evidenced by the previous chapter, proposed definitions that ranged
from the extremely subjective or psychic concepts to the more practical
or real income concepts. Accountants proposed definitions that, in the
broadest sense, approached the economic concept of real income to the
narrow money income concept, which reflects only realized increases

---

[2] William A. Paton, *Accounting*, pp. 1-2.

in the monetary valuation of resources. The courts provided definitions that concentrated on the idea of a "gain" being regarded as income. For example, the U. S. Supreme Court in the famous *Eisner* v. *Macomber* case clarified its position from previous decisions (*Stratton's Independence* v. *Houbert,* 231 U. S. 339, 415 and *Doyle* v. *Mitchell Brothers Company,* 247 U. S. 179, 195) :

Income may be defined as the gain derived from capital, from labor, or from both combined, provided it be understood to include profit gained through a sale or conversion of capital assets . . . .[3]

This decision crystalized the past vague interpretations of the courts and gave the business community a framework for developing accounting concepts of income that would be acceptable for tax purposes, even though the Revenue Act of 1918 had recognized that "net income of a taxpayer computed in accordance with the method of accounting regularly employed" was an acceptable basis for taxable income.

ACCRUAL ACCOUNTING

Although not specifically required, federal income taxation encouraged accountants and businessmen to use the accrual basis of income determination. This encouragement made it necessary for those businesses that adopted the accrual basis to match revenues with appropriate expenses in ascertaining taxable income.[4]

As early as 1918 the tax regulations allowed taxpayers to use accrual accounting for income determination:

Gains, profits, and income are to be included in gross income for the taxable year in which they are received . . . unless they are included when they accrue . . . in accordance with the approved method of accounting followed by the taxpayer.[5]

This emphasis on accrual accounting was subsequently repeated in the

---

[3] *Eisner* v. *Macomber,* 252 (U.S.) 183 (1920).

[4] George O. May, "Taxable Income and Accounting Bases for Determining It," pp. 250-51.

[5] The 1918 Regulation 45, Article 52, quoted in Charles J. Gaa, *The Taxation of Corporate Income,* p. 48.

regulations in 1921 and 1924 and has remained substantially the same even though at times tax methods have deviated from what is considered "good" accounting procedure. Despite these deviations, it is generally agreed that the acceptance and encouragement of accrual accounting by the tax authorities was a major factor contributing to the development and widespread use of the matching concept in the business community. As a result, the groundwork both in theory, such as Paton's popularization and expansion of the entity and going-concern postulates, and in tax regulations and laws was being laid for the ascendancy of the income statement to a position as the primary accounting report for stockholders and other external parties. The only catalyst needed was the previously mentioned fluctuations in prices and the newly emerging investors' viewpoint.

DEPRECIATION

Federal tax laws had a noticeable effect upon other accounting theories and practices which resulted in an increased emphasis on income accounting. For example, the tax law, more than any other factor, probably was responsible for the change in attitude of the business community with respect to the theory that accrued depreciation of fixed assets was a current expense.

Before the 1913 federal tax law, depreciation, if recorded at all, was widely viewed as a valuation concept.[6] Systematic depreciation methods had been devised much earlier than this time. For example, the straight-line, reducing balance, sinking fund and annuity methods, and the unit cost method were not unknown in 1913.[7] After the 1913 tax law, however, depreciation became an important item particularly because it was an allowable deduction for income tax purposes. Paton in commenting on this new emphasis on depreciation said:

Before the days of income taxation it was very difficult for the accountant to convince the businessman, especially the owner of a small enterprise, that it was important for the value expiration of his fixed assets to be accrued upon his books. Now he appears to appreciate the significance of accrued depreciation very clearly, and no urging is required to induce him to book a liberal allowance.[8]

---

[6] Eldon S. Hendrickson, *Accounting Theory*, p. 31.

[7] Earl A. Saliers, *Principles of Depreciation*, pp. 134-73.

[8] William A. Paton, *Accounting Theory*, p. 14.

Upon passage of the 1913 tax law, the subject of the proper accounting for depreciation immediately became a question of controversy. The tax laws have consistently required the cost basis employing the straight-line or units of production methods.[9] Yet, as mentioned above, there were those who viewed depreciation essentially as a valuation concept. For example, the 1913 law permitted depreciation deductions as follows:

Section IIB (Individuals) that in computing net income for the purpose of normal tax there shall be allowed as deductions: a reasonable allowance for the exhaustion, wear and tear of property arising out of its use or employment in the business.... Section IIB (Corporations) .... All losses actually sustained within the year and not compensated by insurance or otherwise, including a reasonable allowance for depreciation by use, wear and tear of property, if any .... [10]

The tax law of 1916 left most of the provisions for depreciation as they were in 1913. But the Act of 1918 made one notable change—it included "a reasonable allowance for obsolescence"[11] in addition to exhaustion, wear, and tear. Prior to this time it was necessary to dispose of property to claim a loss due to obsolescence. In addition, Article 161, Regulation 45 states:

A reasonable allowance for the exhaustion, wear and tear and obsolescence of property used in the trade or business may be deducted from the gross income. For convenience such allowance will be referred to as covering depreciation, excluding from the term any idea of a mere *reduction in the market* value not resulting from exhaustion, wear and tear and obsolescence. The proper allowance for such depreciation ... is the amount which should be set aside for the taxable year in accordance with a consistent plan by which the aggregate of such amounts for the useful life of the property in the business will suffice, with the salvage value, at the end of such useful life to provide in the place of the property its *cost,* or its value as of March 1, 1913, if acquired by the taxpayer before that date.[12]

Here the regulations specifically indicated that a depreciation deduction cannot be based solely on declining market value. On the other hand, cost or March 1, 1913 value is deemed the acceptable basis. The

---

[9] The 1954 code allows accelerated methods of depreciation.
[10] U.S. Government, *Underwood-Simmons Tariff Law,* 1913, Regulations 33.
[11] U.S. Government, *Revenue Act of 1918,* Section 214 (a-7).
[12] Ibid., Article 161, Regulation 45. (Italic added for emphasis.)

Revenue Act of 1924 contained the same provisions with minor exceptions:

Sec. 204 . . . (c) The basis upon which depletion, exhaustion, wear and tear and obsolescence are to be allowed in respect of any property shall be the same basis as is provided in subsection (a) or (b) for the purpose of determining the gain or loss upon the sale or the disposition of property . . . .[13]

Subsection (a) in the above quotation permitted the cost basis if the property was acquired after February 28, 1913. Section (b) allowed cost or value at March 1, 1913, whichever is greater. With the exception of the March 1, 1913 value or cost, whichever is the greater provision, the cost basis for depreciation was clearly expressed. In fact, subsequent tax laws also clearly required the cost basis for the calculation of depreciation.

Even though the tax laws consistently required the cost basis for the calculation of depreciation allowances, there existed some confusion, at least in early tax laws, among the business community and the tax authorities as to the responsibility for ascertaining all the facts necessary for a proper determination of the amount of depreciation. Generally, the tax authorities had prepared the necessary schedules and had been placed in the position of having to demonstrate "clear and convincing" evidence that the taxpayers' claim was unreasonable.[14] This policy of the Internal Revenue tended to slow the development of accurate and detailed records that had originally been started with the passage of the 1913 law. In February 1934 the treasury issued *Treasury Decision 4422* which reversed this policy. This decision was clarified and expanded in 1934 and 1936 as *Mimeograph 4170* and issued by the Bureau of Internal Revenue. A quotation from the 1936 revision reflected this change in policy:

Treasury Decision 4422 approved February 28, 1934, provides that taxpayers claiming deductions from gross income for depreciation furnish full and complete information regarding (1) the cost or other basis of assets for which depreciation is claimed, (2) the age, condition and remaining useful life of the asset, (3) the proportion of the cost or other basis which has been recovered through depreciation allowances for prior taxable years, and (4) such other information as may be required to establish the correctness of the deduction or to determine the amount of the deduction properly allowable . . . .

---

[13] U.S. Government, *Revenue Act of 1924,* Section 204 (c) .
[14] Eugene L. Grant and Paul T. Norton, Jr., *Depreciation,* p. 212.

One of the principal purposes of Treasury Decision 4422 is to place the burden of proof of the correctness of deductions claimed for depreciation squarely upon the taxpayer . . . .[15]

This change in philosophy was the catalyst that was necessary to encourage the recording of depreciation in the accounts on a cost basis. Taxpayers now clearly had the responsibility of keeping adequate accounting records for depreciation based upon cost. M. E. Peloubet, in commenting on *Treasury Decision 4422,* emphasized this point by stating that the "best position for the taxpayer to be in regarding depreciation . . . is to have a detailed record of each item included in his accounts for buildings, machinery and equipment or other depreciable assets showing cost or basis, date acquired, expected life, depreciation written off and all pertinent data." Furthermore, he wrote "the further the taxpayer departs from these conditions the more difficulty he may have in establishing his position."[16] The possibility of the loss of allowances and the fear of tax suits made the calculation of depreciation based on costs a necessary function to be performed by accountants.

In summary, the effect of taxation upon depreciation accounting resulted in the recording of depreciation based on cost. This practice helped to create what Littleton calls the balance sheet dilemma. That is to say, circumstances in the early part of this century, such as rising prices and the wave of mergers and consolidations, resulted in much importance being attached to the balance sheet as a statement of values. But, on the other hand, this emphasis on valuation created problems for the determination of income, such as recognition of revenue before realization. As a result, the cost basis was deemed more appropriate for income determination. Since the tax laws generally favored the purely cost or outlay methods for income determination, businessmen tended to adopt them in their accounts. As a result, the status of the balance sheet as a statement of values decreased, whereas the income statement grew in importance.

INVENTORIES

One of the most significant features in accounting for inventories or

---

[15] U. S. Government, Treasury Department, *Mimeograph 4170 (Revised),* p. 1.

[16] M. E. Peloubet, "Depreciation Under the Revenue Act of 1934," pp. 184-85.

stock in trade has been the emphasis placed upon cost or other input value calculations that are matched against revenue in determining income. This emphasis upon the matching concept placed the accountant in the previously mentioned balance sheet dilemma. Specifically, the matching of cost and revenues resulted in inventory procedures that did not produce the values desired by those using balance sheets for credit purposes.

Federal taxation with respect to inventories, among other things such as the growth of the corporation and price fluctuations, was a primary factor influencing this emphasis on the matching concept. Paton, once again, recognized this influence as early as 1922. For example, he stated:

> The influence of the closing inventory balance upon the exhibits of net incomes ... is of such consequence as to call for the most searching scrutiny of inventory practices and an insistence upon the use of rational and accurate principles and procedures. Particularly in these days of serious tax levies upon incomes and profits has the entire inventory process become a matter of the utmost importance to all concerned. The businessman can no longer be satisfied with an inventory, calculated by the cubic yard, for example ....[17]

Tax laws and various regulations initially favored specific identification of costs with revenues as the method for allocating inventory to cost of goods sold for income determination. But the 1918 regulations accepted the first-in, first-out method of allocating costs between inventories and cost of goods sold.[18] The FIFO method was accepted primarily because it yielded a good approximation of the results obtained under specific identification. In addition, it was felt that FIFO combined all elements of profit and recognized them at the time of sale, that is, it did not permit the recognition of unrealized gains and losses. Furthermore, it resulted in the presentation of ending inventory balances at the most recent cost for balance sheet purposes.[19] This acceptance of the FIFO method by the tax authorities tended to favor those who espoused the balance sheet as a statement of values for credit purposes.

The widespread use of FIFO resulted in various attempts by those advocating the matching concept to point out its inadequacies for use

---

[17] William A. Paton, "Valuation of Inventories," *Journal of Accountancy*, p. 432.

[18] 1918, Regulation 45, Article 1582.

[19] Hendrickson, *Accounting Theory*, p. 269.

in the matching of current costs with current revenues. For example, a publication by the American Institute of Accountants contained a statement that opposed the traditional belief that the flow of costs should follow the flow of goods:

> ... it may not be a matter of great importance whether cost of goods on hand is determined on the theory that the first goods in are the first goods to go out, or that the last goods in are the first to go out.[20]

This statement, along with the standard arguments relative to variations in periodic profits resulting from use of FIFO, was employed in attempts to justify the use of the LIFO method. As a result of these efforts, the Internal Revenue Code was changed in 1939 and in 1947 a tax court confirmed the acceptance of LIFO.[21] These actions left the door open for all taxpayers to use LIFO in their accounts. The final downfall of the balance sheet as a statement of values or near value was now completed. The income objective prevailed.

INFLUENCE OF THE SECURITIES AND EXCHANGE COMMISSION

Background

The legislation leading to the formation of the SEC in the 1930s was not a spontaneous reaction to the depression. In fact, there is evidence that this legislation had many historical antecedents. Particularly, some contend that the laws were directed toward the financial practices of a prosperity period rather than those found more often in a depression era.[22] Time and time again the financial scandals and malpractices of the late 1920s were discussed in 1933 and 1934 before the Senate Committee on Banking and Currency by experts in accounting, business, and law. In short, the passage of the Securi-

---

[20] American Institute of Accountants, *Examination of Financial Statements by Independent Public Accountants*, p. 3.

[21] Hutzler Brothers, 8th Tax Court 14, 1947.

[22] J. R. Taylor, "Some Antecedents of the Securities and Exchange Commission," p. 188.

ties Act of 1933 and the Securities Exchange Act of 1934 reflected the public awareness of the emerging investors' point of view. In addition, not only the specific requirements of these acts were important, but the fear of regulation tended to produce improvements in financial reporting practices.

SCOPE OF FEDERAL SECURITIES LAWS

Commerce Clearing House, Inc. stated in its review of the securities laws:

The federal securities laws govern companies that seek to acquire new capital by the issuance of securities to the public, and persons in the business of buying and selling securities.... They are designed to protect the interest of investors and the public by certain disclosure requirements and by prohibiting fraud and manipulative practices.[23]

This statement clearly reflected the fact that the new investors' viewpoint had found expression in legislative acts. The laws required the securities issuer to make available to potential investors certain information about the issuer and the securities offered including, among other things, the plan of distribution, use of proceeds, capital structure, summary of earnings, organization, affiliations, description of businesses and property, pending legal proceedings, and financial statements.[24] The registration requirements as set forth in the laws, particularly with respect to the nature and form of financial statements, indicated the new emphasis accorded the income statement. For example, Schedule A (25) of the Securities Act of 1933 states that:

...a balance sheet as of a date not more than ninety days prior to the date of filing the registration statement showing all the assets of the issuer, the nature and *cost* thereof, whenever determinable, in such detail and in such form as the Commission shall prescribe, including, *surplus* of the issuer showing how and from what sources such surplus was created, all as of a date not more than ninety days prior to the filing of the registration statement....[25]

---

[23] Commerce Clearing House, *Federal Securities Law Reports,* p. 101.

[24] Ibid., p. 104.

[25] U.S. Government, *Securities Act of 1933,* an act of May 27, 1933, Schedule A (25).

This statement, although for the balance sheet, implied that the income objective is more significant for at least two reasons. First, the reference to assets recorded on a cost basis, as stated before, was the condition considered necessary for the matching concept. In other words, this view is supported by those who believed that the balance sheet was a residual statement and reflected cost awaiting assignment to revenue. The second point is the reference to the surplus account of the issuer. This also reflected the increased emphasis on income accounting since it was considered necessary to identify the sources from which a surplus was created.

Schedule A (25) referred to the registration requirement of the income statement as follows:

... a profit and loss statement of the issuer showing earnings and income, the nature and source thereof, and the expenses and fixed charges in such detail and such form as the Commission shall prescribe for the latest fiscal year for which statement is available and for the two preceding fiscal years, year by year, or .... Such statement shall show what the practice of the issuer has been during the three years or lesser period as to the character of the charges, dividends or other distributions made against the surplus accounts, and as to depreciation, depletion, and maintenance charges, in such detail and form as the Commission shall prescribe .... [26]

This quotation is important because it demonstrated the extent the law required income statement data. Information as to depreciation, expenses, and distributions against the surplus accounts was seldom disclosed in published annual reports prior to this time.[27] Because of the passage of this law, companies included this information in annual reports since it was made public by the disclosure requirements contained in the law. As a result, income statement data appeared in annual reports, corresponding to the emergence of income reporting that was documented in chapter three.

THE SECURITIES EXCHANGE ACT OF 1934

The Securities Exchange Act of 1934, like the 1933 act, was designed to protect the investing public. Under this act, registration

---

[26] Ibid., Schedule A (26).
[27] T. H. Sanders, "Influence of the Securities and Exchange Commission upon Accounting Principles," pp. 73-74.

was necessary by any company that sought to acquire new capital by the issuance of securities to the public. Also, this act required that financial data be kept current by means of periodic reports attested to by independent public accountants.[28]

Under this act, the SEC has broad powers to specify the form and content of financial statements and other reports required to be filed. It has specific authority to require the following:

The Commission may prescribe ... the form or forms in which the required information shall be set forth, the items or details to be shown in the balance sheet and the earnings statement, and the methods to be followed in the preparation of reports, in the appraisal or valuation of assets and liabilities, in the determination of depreciation and depletion, in the differentiation of recurring and nonrecurring income, in the differentiation of investment and operating income ....[29]

The above statement indicated that the SEC had the authority to prescribe accounting procedures and the form of financial statements. Also, it is obvious that this authority encompassed specific areas that are very relevant to a proper matching of costs with revenues, such as depreciation, recurring and non-recurring items, and differentiation between capital and income. But the specific recommendations were essentially left to the accounting profession, even though the latter group was very much influenced by the policies of the SEC. As is now known, the accounting profession developed principles of accounting that reflected the attention directed to the income statement.

ACCOUNTING SERIES RELEASES—REGULATION S-X

The Securities and Exchange Commission in 1937 began a program of publication of opinions on accounting principles for the purpose of contributing to the development of more uniform standards for financial statements. These opinions are found in the *Accounting Series Releases and Regulation S-X*, which stated the requirements for financial statements filed with the commission as prescribed under the various acts.

---

[28] Commerce Clearing House, *Law Reports*, II 20, 332-33.
[29] *U.S. Government, Securities Exchange Act of 1934*, an act of June 6, 1934, Section 13 (b).

On April 25, 1935 the SEC stated its administrative policy with respect to financial statements that reflected the dependence placed upon the accounting profession.

In cases where financial statements filed with this Commission pursuant to its rules and regulations under the Securities Act of 1933 or the Securities Exchange Act of 1934 are prepared in accordance with accounting principles for which there is no substantial authoritative support, such financial statements will be presumed to be misleading or inaccurate despite disclosures contained in the certificate of the accountant or in footnotes to the statements provided the matters involved are material. In cases where there is a difference of opinion between the Commission and the registrant as to the proper principles of accounting to be followed, disclosure will be accepted in lieu of correction of the financial statements themselves only if the points involved are such that there is substantial authoritative support for the practices followed by the registrant and the position of the Commission has not previously been expressed in rules, regulations, or other official releases of the Commission, including the published opinions of the chief accountant.[30]

This statement of policy is significant because it enhanced the status of the American Institute of Accountants and its opinions on relevant accounting issues. Thus, subsequent opinions by the institute on accounting principles, emphasizing the importance of the income statement, were carefully reviewed and heeded by the business community. George O. May supported this view even though he believed the formulation of the commission was unnecessary:

Its [SEC] decisions on general accounting questions have usually been reached after consultation with the Institute, its influence on accounting practice in the field of general business has undoubtedly been beneficial. However, this benefit has arisen from the enforcement of rules which were laid down prior to its creation, and from strengthening the position of the accountant in relation to the corporation rather than from the formulation of new rules.[31]

SUMMARY

This chapter discussed the influence of taxation and other govern-

---

[30] U.S. Securities and Exchange Commission, "Release No. 4: Administrative Policy on Financial Statements," *Accounting Series Releases* (Washington, D.C.: U.S. Government Printing Office, 1936), pp. 5-6.
[31] George O. May, *Financial Accounting: A Distillation of Experience* (New York: The Macmillan Company, 1943), p. 67.

ment legislation on the shift in emphasis from the balance sheet to the income statement by external parties. It was concluded that the passage of the Sixteenth Amendment and subsequent legislation led businessmen to consider it imperative that profit figures be calculated with the greatest possible degree of precision. As a result, accountants began to focus attention on the determination of periodic income.

Federal income taxation encouraged accountants to use the actual basis for income determination. This led to increased attention to the matching of revenues with expenses within a specific time period. Depreciation and inventory accounting for the purpose of calculating taxable income were contributing factors to the external shift in emphasis. The tax laws consistently required that depreciation and inventories be calculated on a cost basis for the purposes of ascertaining taxable income. This led to the adoption of the cost basis for general accounting and to the balance sheet dilemma, that is, to the controversy between those who felt the balance sheet should represent a statement of values and those who felt it should be based upon cost.

The legislation leading to the formation of the Securities and Exchange Commission, the Securities Act of 1933, and the Securities Exchange Act of 1934, also was an important force contributing to the external shift, especially in corporate reporting. This legislation was important because it reflected the new investors' viewpoint and it prompted the accounting profession to undertake extensive research focused on those principles underlying the preparation of financial statements.

5

Summary and Conclusions

This study in the history of accounting thought identifies the nature of the shift in emphasis from the balance sheet to the income statement as the primary accounting report. The more important forces responsible for this ascendancy of the income statement utilized an historical approach based upon the interpretation of evidence resulting from the interaction of ideas and events. This historical approach was based upon (1) a type of research or inquiry designed to answer questions; (2) an attempt to discover human beings' actions that occurred in the past; (3) a process by which evidence is interpreted; and (4) a means whereby perspective could be provided for making choices today. In historical research the historian is confronted with many problems. There is first the problem of his raw materials as much of the past was never recorded. Another problem relates to the fact that bias distorts his view; but bias can be effectively handled by revealing the raw materials used, by explicitly stating the organizational scheme, and by revealing the standards that condition the historian's interpretations.

In this study, old corporate annual reports, selected accounting literature, correspondence and internal income statements from selected companies, governmental publications and legislative acts, and interviews, where appropriate, were the basic raw materials. The organizational scheme was to determine the interrelationships between past ideas and events influencing accounting actions. Under this approach both exogenous and endogenous environmental variables can be related to the study.

Contemporary accounting theory was used as a framework for making judgments necessary to interpret past accounting actions that may have contributed to the matching concept as it is known today. It also served as a basis for demonstrating the continued interaction between accounting and economics. Furthermore, contemporary accounting theory was valuable particularly because accounting actions of the past could be viewed through its lens. For example, those forces contributing to the decline of the balance sheet as a statement of values could be easily identified since it was known that the cost principle eventually emerged.

The conclusion reached in chapters two and three was that there are essentially two shifts in emphasis from balance sheet data to income statement data. There is an internal or managerial shift and an external shift by stockholders, creditors, and other parties outside the firm. The former shift probably occurred with the advent of the corporate form of business organization, characterized by the separation of owners and managers, between 1880 and 1925. On the other hand, the latter shift began in the 1920s, accelerated in the 1930s, and was essentially completed by the early 1940s.

The internal shift in emphasis was more difficult to document than was the external shift. Information was obtained in the form of letters, internal income statements, interviews, or combinations of all three from various selected companies. This information related to the nature and extent of internal income reporting prior to the external shift in emphasis. From this information it was concluded that there was no significant internal shift in emphasis in the early 1930s. Income reporting was considered very important to management for the purpose of testing the profitability of operations as a guide to future action long before the advent of the external shift.

The most probable force that set the chain of ideas and events into motion leading to the emergence of income statement data in managerial decisions was the sudden increase in inventions appearing in England shortly after 1750, even though these inventions were themselves the result of many complex and remote causes. These inventions helped pave the way for the industrialization of society through the use of the factory system. It now became necessary to accumulate large amounts of capital to meet the technical requirements for mass production. In addition, the industrialization of society increased the degree of competition which made survival tenuous at best. As a result, a system based on partnerships or joint-stock companies emerged which was called Industrial Capitalism.

The great industrial capitalists were specialists in production rather than finance and followed a social code from the philosophy of Social Darwinism. Financial mechanisms, such as balance sheets and income statements, were despised by the industrial capitalist. Yet much emphasis was placed on efficiency as measured by the increase in the physical volume of output (for example, tons of steel).

In the last quarter of the nineteenth century the state of technological progress, the increasing demand for mass produced goods, and the bitterly competitive atmosphere that the industrial capitalists had produced with their ruthless tactics created a need for a new type of business organization. The corporation with its features of stock ownership, limited liability, transferability of interests, and separation of owners and managers was ideally suited to fulfill this need.

The financial capitalist—the banker, the investment banker, and the insurance company—initiated the corporate revolution in America. The financial capitalist was not interestd in the day-to-day operations of the business since he spread his interests over many different industries. Therefore, managers were appointed to assume this function. As a result, a new professional managerial class emerged.

The professional manager was a specialist who depended upon accounting, statistical, and economic data in making decisions. Since he was held responsible for his performance and since competition was keen, he needed to test the profitability of operations as a guide for future actions and did so through the use of cost and revenue data. The development of cost accounting and the work of the scientific engineers between 1885 and 1930 provided evidential support for this internal shift in emphasis. Furthermore, a survey of selected companies indicated that profit and loss data were accumulated and used internally long before the external shift in emphasis occurred in the early 1930s.

The external shift in emphasis was the result of many forces. Like the internal shift, the rise of the corporation was very important. It prompted Paton and others to focus attention on the entity concept and the going-concern assumption. The emergence of the investors' viewpoint resulting from the rapid growth of stock ownership by the general public resulted in a new demand for information. Investors sought growth as well as the safety of their original investment. The income statement was useful for this purpose because it yielded profit data very essential in analyzing investment alternatives.

The rapid fluctuation in the price of goods and services that began in the early 1920s left doubt in the public's mind as to the adequacy of the balance sheet as a statement of values. But federal taxation of income and related court decisions were the most important developments contributing to the emergence of income reporting via the matching concept. Federal tax laws have consistently required the cost basis for such items as depreciation and inventories. This requirement naturally contributed to the demise of the balance sheet as a statement of values and its replacement with a statement of unallocated or residual costs. The courts played a key role in the emergence of the matching because they became involved with the problem of identifying what was income. In the famous decision of *Eisner* v. *Macomber* it was held that income did not exist until it was severed from capital. This meant that for most types of property, income could emerge only through the sale or exchange of the property. Thus, accountants concentrated on rules and procedures that would identify a severance or sale of assets. As a result the transactions approach to income determination based upon the realization concept emerged.

The main point in this study is that accounting evolution involves the interaction of ideas and events which change a permanent feature. It demonstrated the futility of arguing about how progress in accounting proceeds since both practice and theory interact to cause change. Those forces considered to be primarily responsible for both the external and internal shift in emphasis involved developments in accounting practice and theory, and exogenous changes in other disciplines. For an appropriate perspective in making decisions, one should be cognizant of these forces. For example, one of the major reasons for the external shift was the emergence of the investors' viewpoint resulting from the corporate revolution. Investors demanded information that was useful in ascertaining the relative profitability of various investment alternatives. The income statement was an excellent means for supplying this information.

Today the environment has changed. Corporations have evolved into a new dimension—conglomerates. The conventional net income is no longer as significant to investors. Information is being demanded concerning the profitability of divisions and product lines. Once again the SEC is interested in seeing that these new investor demands are met. As a result, the accounting profession, if it is to maintain its autonomy, must take an active role in providing the kinds of information demanded.

The shift in emphasis also clearly shows the importance of specifying objectives. This involves an understanding of not only the types of information demanded, but also a general knowledge of the groups demanding the information. The consequences of emphasizing the creditor viewpoint in determining the type of information supplied by accountants were revealed. Objectives of accounting should not only consider creditors, but managers, investors, and other outside interested parties as well should be considered.

Furthermore, the identification in this study of certain significant ideas and events influencing accounting actions of the past provided perspective for analyzing current movements and trends. For example, one significant trend is the attempt to make the balance sheet a better tool for valuation and income determination. One of the leading proponents of this view is R. J. Chambers. He states:

It is contended . . . that the swing from the balance sheet viewpoint to the profit and loss viewpoint has gone too far. It has gone so far, it is believed, because of the desire to bolster conventional accounting methods. In changing conditions the conventional profit and loss account gives a better approximation to current net profit than the conventional balance sheet gives to current financial position. If one claims that the profit and loss account is the most important statement, one can make light of the defects of the conventional balance sheet. . . .

It does not follow from the statement "earning power is the significant basis of enterprise value" that "the income statement is the most significant accounting report." The income statement does not show earning power; it shows earnings. Earning power is only ascertainable from a comparison of earnings with the sum employed; net profit of itself is not significant. It follows that the income account and the balance sheet are of equal importance for this purpose, and that the further the asset values move from invested cost without restatement of those values and of the shareholder's equity, the greater is the distortion of the current relationship between net profit and the sum employed.[1]

In his book, *Accounting, Evaluation and Economic Behavior,* a case is made for the reinstatement of the balance sheet as the primary accounting report. Chambers compares business entities to individuals as "homeostatic systems" being influenced by a host of factors, including economic phenomenon. The condition which has the greatest influence on the choices of an actor, as he describes it, is his "present position in relation to his environment at any point of time." In fact, this position "is the determinant and predictor of future positions, as it is also the resultant of past positions." Knowing this position is a

---

[1] Raymond J. Chambers, "The Implications of Asset Revaluation and Bonus Share Issues," pp. 514-15.

necessary, but not a sufficient, condition for successful choosing or acting.[2] To business entities it is financial position as reflected in the balance sheet that serves as the basis for successful choosing or acting. The income statement "is derived, fundamentally, by reference from two successive statements of financial position."[3] As a result, the income statement is reduced in importance while the balance sheet is elevated in importance. That is to say, the capital maintenance approach to income determination is adopted.

Chambers is decisively different than economists with respect to his valuation concept used for income calculations. He generally adopts what is called the "current cash equivalent" basis for valuation as opposed to capitalized values based upon expectations. For example he states:

Calculations about future conditions and events are always and inevitably hypothetical. No proposition relating to the future is a statement of fact. One may use past experience and present knowledge of facts and relationships in forming propositions about the future. But those propositions are beliefs or expectations only.[4]

It seems that future expectations are most relevant. Current prices under pure competition reflect the interaction of supply and demand forces. One of the most important forces that influence these prices are expectations. Thus, current prices are significant, as Chambers suggests, under perfect markets because they reflect expectations, not just because they are objective. In imperfect markets current prices are significant only because they represent the lowest minimum subjective value to an actor contemplating a purchase. For example, a businessman would not be willing to purchase a machine if its discounted value to him is less than its market price. In short, the principle of capitalization based upon expectations is essential to the whole problem of valuation, which in turn is the basis for action. Thus, valuation is subjective. Resulting income calculations are tentative and uncertain. To the extent the current cash equivalents approximate capitalized values then they are relevant to accounting because they meet the other standards of verifiability, freedom from bias, and

---

[2] Raymond J. Chambers, *Accounting, Evaluation and Economic Behavior*, pp. 80-81.

[3] Ibid., p. 118.

[4] Ibid., p. 83.

quantifiability as proposed by the American Accounting Association.

Another significant trend is the movement toward revising the meaning of the realization concept in an effort to provide better income data and to upgrade the status of the balance sheet. Traditionally the time of sale has been the general rule for the recognition or realization of revenue, because it is argued that (1) the price of the product is now established, (2) an exchange or new asset has been acquired, (3) the sale in most instances is deemed to be the most significant event to a firm, and (4) most of the costs relating to the product have been incurred and are readily determinable.[5] In short, the general view is that realization is the recognition of revenue when an exchange or severance has occurred.

The effect of this strict adherence to the realization concept is that traditional accounting income does not recognize (1) changes in net assets not realized in the period (such as value added approach), (2) changes in price levels, (3) unexpected changes in expectations, and (4) expected changes in goodwill.[6] With the possible exception of unexpected changes in expectations, economists take into consideration all these factors when calculating income.

Today the traditional realization concept is under attack as evidenced by the volumes of literature. R. S. Sprouse and M. Moonitz reject the concept because it is in conflict with the postulate of continuity.[7] Instead they advocate that recognition should be granted in the period in which the major economic activity occurred, providing objective measurements of this activity are available.[8] The American Accounting Association has likewise broadened the meaning of realization to include "a change in an asset or liability" if it is "sufficiently definite and objective to warrant recognition in the accounts." Thus realization can result from "an exchange transaction between independent parties, or on established trade practices, or on the terms of a contract performance of which is considered to be virtually certain."[9]

---

[5] Hendrickson, *Accounting Theory*, p. 138.

[6] Emily Chen Chang, "Business Income in Accounting and Economics," *Accounting Review*, October 1962, p. 641.

[7] Robert S. Sprouse and Maurice Moonitz, "A Tentative Set of Broad Accounting Principles for Business Enterprises," p. 15.

[8] Ibid., p. 47.

[9] American Accounting Association Committee on Accounting Concepts and Standards, *Accounting and Reporting Standards for Corporate Financial Statements and Preceding Statements and Supplements*, p. 3.

According to Floyd W. Windal, the American Accounting Association definition of realization is broadly stated and equally applicable to expenses, gains and losses, and other changes in assets and liabilities. For example, he stated that "the key point is whether a change in an asset or liability, presumably any change, has become sufficiently definite and objective to warrant recognition in the accounts."[10] He considered an item objective if it appeared "substantially the same to all accountants examining it." By definiteness an item "must appear unlikely to be reversed."[11] Furthermore, in his concluding remarks Windal suggested that the criteria for realization may change with time. In fact, computers, economic structures, and economic stability "may make it possible to forecast with great certainty what lies ahead for an enterprise."[12]

From the above statements relative to the realization concept, there is evidence that accountants are relaxing the strict requirements of the traditional view. The result is that many contend income accounting should recognize changes in net assets not "realized" in the period if objective verifiable evidence exists, and gains and losses from price movements, both general and relative. Thus, the difference between economic income and accounting income is narrowed to changes in expectations and expected changes in goodwill. If computers, economic structures, economic stability, and fiscal policy continue to reduce uncertainty, then it might be possible to use probability values in accounting calculations, thus narrowing the area of disagreement even more. Furthermore, it is felt that concentration on valuation and measurement theory can also reduce the difference. The problem should not be the balance sheet versus the income statement approach to income calculations because valuation of assets and liabilities in the former is merely shifted to the valuation of assets and liabilities entering and leaving the firm in the latter. Both approaches yield identical results under appropriate valuation methods and identical assumptions.

---

[10] Floyd W. Windal, "The Accounting Concept of Realization," p. 250.
[11] Ibid., p. 252.
[12] Ibid., p. 208.

Bibliography

BOOKS

American Accounting Association. *Accounting and Reporting Standards for Corporate Financial Statements and Preceding Statements and Supplements.* Columbus, Ohio: American Accounting Association, 1957.

———. *A Statement of Basic Accounting Theory.* Evanston, Ill.: American Accounting Association, 1966.

American Institute of Accountants. *Audits of Corporate Accounts.* New York: American Institute of Accountants, 1934.

———. *Changing Concepts of Business Income.* New York: The Macmillan Co., 1952.

———. *Examination of Financial Statements by Independent Public Accountants.* New York: American Institute Publishing Co., 1936.

Baldwin, James Mark. *Dictionary of Philosophy and Psychology*. New York: The Macmillan Co., 1955.

Blaug, M. *Economic Theory in Retrospect*. Homewood, Ill.: Richard D. Irwin, 1962.

Burns, Edward McNall. *Western Civilizations*. New York: W. W. Norton and Co., 1958.

Canning, John B. *The Economics of Accountancy*. New York: The Ronald Press Co., 1929.

Chambers, Raymond J. *Accounting, Evaluation and Economic Behavior*. Englewood Cliffs, N. J.: Prentice-Hall, 1966.

Clark, John Bates. *The Distribution of Wealth*. New York: The Macmillan Co., 1899.

Cole, William Morse. *Accounts, Their Construction and Interpretation*. New York: Houghton Mifflin Co., 1908.

Collingwood, R. G. *The Idea of History*. London: Oxford University Press, 1946.

Commager, Henry. *The Study of History*. Columbus, Ohio: Charles E. Merrill Books, 1965.

Commerce Clearing House. *Federal Securities Law Reports*. New York: Commerce Clearing House, 1967.

Copi, Irving M. *Introduction to Logic*. 2d ed. New York: The Macmillan Co., 1961.

Corey, Lewis. *The House of Morgan*. New York: Grosset and Dunlap, 1930.

Couchman, Chester B. *The Balance Sheet*. New York: *The Journal of Accountancy*, 1923.

Davenport, Herbert Joseph. *The Economics of Enterprise*. New York: The Macmillan Co., 1913.

Deinzer, Harvey T. *Development of Accounting Thought.* New York: Holt, Rinehart and Winston, 1965.

Edwards, Edgar O., and Bell, Philip W. *The Theory and Measurement of Business Income.* Los Angeles: University of California Press, 1965.

Edwards, James Don. *History of Public Accounting in the United States.* East Lansing: Bureau of Business and Economic Research, Graduate School of Business Administration, Michigan State University, 1960.

Edwards, Paul, ed. *The Encyclopedia of Philosophy.* New York: The Macmillan Co., 1967.

Fisher, Irving. *Elementary Principles of Economics.* New York: The Macmillan Co., 1911.

————. *The Nature of Capital and Income.* New York: The Macmillan Co., 1906.

Gaa, Charles J. *The Taxation of Corporate Income.* Urbana: University of Illinois Press, 1944.

Galbraith, John Kenneth. *The Affluent Society.* Boston: Houghton Mifflin Co., 1958.

————. *The Great Crash.* Boston: Houghton Mifflin Co., 1961.

Garner, S. Paul. *Evolution of Cost Accounting to 1925.* University: University of Alabama Press, 1954.

General Electric Company. *General Electric's Growth.* Book One. General Electric Co., 1953.

Gide, Charles, and Rist, Charles. *A History of Economic Doctrines.* 2d ed. New York: D. C. Heath and Co., 1949.

Gilman, Stephen. *Accounting Concepts of Profit.* New York: The Ronald Press Co., 1939.

Goldberg, Louis. *An Inquiry into the Nature of Accounting.* Monograph No. 7. American Accounting Association, 1964.

Grant, Eugene L., and Norton, Paul T. Jr. *Depreciation.* New York: The Ronald Press Co., 1949.

Grivalli, Pietro. *An Original Translation of the Treatise on Double-Entry.* New York: Harper Brothers, n.d.

Haney, Lewis H. *History of Economic Thought.* 4th ed. New York: The Macmillan Co., 1949.

Hatfield, Henry Rand. *Accounting: Its Principles and Problems.* New York: D. Appleton and Co., 1929.

———. *Modern Accounting.* New York: D. Appleton and Co., 1909.

Hawley, Frederick B. *Enterprise and the Productive Process.* New York: G. P. Putnam's Sons, 1907.

Heckscher, Eli F. *Mercantilism.* 2 vols. London: George Allen and Unwin, 1935.

Hendrickson, Eldon S. *Accounting Theory.* Homewood, Ill.: Richard D. Irwin, 1965.

Hicks, J. R. *Value and Capital: An Inquiry into Some Fundamental Principles of Economic Theory.* 2d ed. Oxford: The Clarendon Press, 1950.

Hobson, J. A. *The Industrial System, an Inquiry into Earned and Unearned Income.* rev. ed. London: P. S. King and Sons, 1910.

Ijiri, Yuji. *The Foundations of Accounting Measurement.* Englewood Cliffs, N. J.: Prentice-Hall, 1967.

Johnson, E. A., and Kroose, Herman E. *The American Economy.* Englewood Cliffs, N. J.: Prentice-Hall, 1960.

Kester, Roy B. *Accounting Theory and Practice.* New York: The Ronald Press Co., 1917.

———. *Accounting Theory and Practice.* New York: The Ronald Press Co., 1930.

Keynes, John Maynard. *A Treatise on Probability.* London: The Macmillan Co., 1948.

Knight, Frank H. *Risk, Uncertainty and Profit.* New York: Kelley and Millman, reprint of 1921 ed., 1952.

Knoeppel, C. E. *Organization and Administration.* New York: Industrial Extension Institute, 1921.

Kroose, Herman E. *American Economic Development.* Englewood Cliffs, N. J.: Prentice-Hall, 1962.

Littleton, A. C. *Accounting Evolution to 1900.* New York: American Institute Publishing Co., 1933.

———. *Essays on Accountancy.* Urbana: University of Illinois Press, 1961.

———. *Structure of Accounting Theory.* Monograph No. 5. Urbana: American Accounting Association, 1953.

Littleton, A. C., and Zimmerman, V. K. *Accounting Theory: Continuity and Change.* Englewood Cliffs, N. J.: Prentice-Hall, 1962.

Malthus, Thomas R. *Principles of Political Economy.* New York: Augustus M. Kelley, reprint of 1820 ed., 1951.

Marshall, Alfred. *Principles of Economics.* 8th ed. London: Macmillan and Co., 1920.

Marx, Karl. *Theories of Surplus Value.* Translated by G. A. Bonner and Emile Burns. New York: International Publishers, 1952.

Mautz, R. K., and Sharaf, Hussein A. *The Philosophy of Auditing.* Monograph No. 6. American Accounting Association, 1966.

May, George O. *Financial Accounting.* New York: The Macmillan Co., 1943.

McConnell, Campbell R. *Economics: Principles, Problems, and Policies.* 2d ed. New York: McGraw-Hill Co., 1963.

McKinsey, James O. *Accounting Principles.* Cincinnati: South-Western Publishing Co., 1929.

McKinsey, James O., and Noble, Howard S. *Accounting Principles.* 2d ed. Cincinnati: South-Western Publishing Co., 1935.

———. *Accounting Principles.* 3d ed. Cincinnati: South-Western Publishing Co., 1939.

Means, Gardiner C. *The Corporate Revolution in America.* New York: The Crowell-Collier Publishing Co., 1962.

Meek, Ronald L. *The Economics of Physiocracy.* Cambridge, Mass.: Harvard University Press, 1963.

Mill, John Stuart. *Principles of Political Economy.* New York: Augustus M. Kelley, reprint of 3d ed. 1852, 1961.

Montgomery, Robert H. *Auditing Theory and Practice.* New York: The Ronald Press Co., 1912.

———. *Auditing Theory and Practice.* 5th ed. The Ronald Press Co., 1934.

———. *Auditing Theory and Practice.* 6th ed. The Ronald Press Co., 1940.

Moonitz, Maurice. *The Basic Postulates of Accounting.* New York: American Institute of Certified Public Accountants, 1961.

Newman, Phillip Charles. *The Development of Economic Thought.* Englewood Cliffs, N. J.: Prentice-Hall, 1952.

Nicholson, J. Lee. *Factory Organization and Costs.* New York: Kohl Technical Publishing Co., 1909.

———. *Profitable Management.* New York: The Ronald Press Co., 1923.

Nicholson, J. Lee, and Rohrback, John F. D. *Cost Accounting.* New York: The Ronald Press Co., 1919.

Noble, Howard S. *Accounting Principles.* 4th ed. Cincinnati: South-Western Publishing Co., 1945.

Paton, William A. *Accounting.* New York: The Macmillan Co., 1926.

―――. *Accounting Theory.* Chicago: Accounting Studies Press, reprint of 1922 ed., 1962.

Paton, W. A., and Littleton, A. C. *An Introduction to Corporate Accounting Standards.* Ann Arbor: American Accounting Association, 1940.

Perangallo, Edward. *Origin and Evolution of Double Entry Bookkeeping.* New York: American Institute Publishing Co., 1938.

Rappaport, Louis H. *SEC Accounting Practice and Procedure.* New York: The Ronald Press Co., 1956.

Ricardo, David. *The Principles of Political Economy and Taxation.* New York: E. P. Dutton and Co., reprint of 1817 ed., 1937.

Ripley, William Z. *Main Street and Wall Street.* Boston: Little, Brown, and Co., 1927.

―――. *Railroads, Finance and Organization.* New York: Longmans, Green and Company, 1915.

Saliers, Earl. *Principles of Depreciation.* New York: The Ronald Press Co., 1915.

Schumpeter, Joseph A. *History of Economic Analysis.* New York: Oxford University Press, 1954.

Sloan, Alfred P., Jr. *My Years with General Motors.* Garden City, N.Y.: Doubleday and Co., 1964.

Smith, Adam. *The Wealth of Nations.* Edited by Edwin Cannan. 2 vols. New Rochelle, N. Y.: Arlington House, reprint of 1776 ed., 1950.

Soloman, Ezra. *The Theory of Financial Management.* New York: Columbia University Press, 1963.

Soule, George. *Soule's New Science and Practice of Accounts.* 7th ed. New Orleans: unknown, 1903.

Sprague, Charles E. *The Philosophy of Accounts.* New York: The Ronald Press Co., 1908.

Sprouse Robert T., and Moonitz, Maurice. "A Tentative Set of Broad Accounting Principles for Business Enterprises," *Accounting Research Study No. 3.* New York: American Institute of Certified Public Accountants, 1962.

Storey, Reed K. *The Search for Accounting Principles.* New York: American Institute of Certified Public Accountants, 1964.

Taussig, F. W. *Principles of Economics.* 2 vols. New York: The Macmillan Co., 1913.

Taylor, Frederick W. *The Principles of Scientific Management.* New York: Harper and Brothers Publishers, 1911.

———. *Shop Management.* New York: Harper and Brothers Publishers, 1911.

Turgot, Anne-Robert-Jacques. *Reflections on the Formation and Distribution of Riches.* New York: The Macmillan Co., reprint of 1776 ed., 1911.

Webner, Frank E. *Factory Costs.* New York: The Ronald Press Co. 1911.

ARTICLES AND PERIODICALS

American Accounting Association. "Accounting Concepts and Standards Underlying Corporate Financial Statements," 1948 Revision, *Accounting Review,* October 1948, pp. 339-44.

———. "Accounting Principles Underlying Corporate Financial Statements," *Accounting Review,* June 1941, pp. 133-39.

———. "A Statement of Objectives of the American Accounting Association," *Accounting Review,* March 1936, pp. 1-4.

———. "A Tentative Statement of Accounting Principles Affecting Corporate Reports," *Accounting Review,* June 1936, pp. 187-91.

Bailey, George D. "The Increasing Significance of the Income Statement," *Journal of Accountancy,* January 1948, pp. 10-19.

Bowers, Russell. "Tests of Income Realization," *Accounting Review,* June 1941, pp. 139-55.

Brundage, P. F. "Influence of Government Regulation on Development of Today's Accounting Practices," *Journal of Accountancy,* November 1950, pp. 384-91.

Chambers, Raymond J. "The Implications of Assets Revaluation and Bonus Share Issues," *Australian Accountant,* November 1957, pp. 507-31.

Chang, Emily Chen. "Business Income in Accounting and Economics," *Accounting Review,* October 1962, pp. 636-44.

Clark, John Bates. "Insurance and Business Profits," *The Quarterly Journal of Economics,* October 1892, pp. 40-54.

———. "Profits Under Modern Conditions," *Political Science Quarterly,* 1887, pp. 603-19.

Daines, H. C., "The Changing Objectives of Accounting," *Accounting Review,* June 1929, pp. 94-110.

DeRooner, Raymond. "The Lingering Influence of Medieval Practices," *Accounting Review,* April 1943, pp. 148-51.

Donald, A. G. "Historical Background of Accounting as a Control," *The Accountants' Digest,* October 1967, pp. 18-20.

Editorial. "Clear Statements Needed," *Journal of Accountancy,* July 1930, pp. 5-7.

———. "Earning Per Share," *Journal of Accountancy,* May 1930, pp. 322-24.

———. "Fruits of Experiment," *Journal of Accountancy,* November 1933, pp. 320-22.

———. "Income Defined at Last," *Journal of Accountancy,* February 1928, pp. 125-27.

———. *Journal of Accountancy,* March 1934, pp. 168-72.

———. "The Meaning of a Balance Sheet," *Journal of Accountancy,* December 1928, pp. 445-46.

———. "What Is Income?" *Journal of Accountancy,* June 1933, pp. 401-2.

———. "What Are Net Profits?" *Journal of Accountancy,* January 1929, pp. 44-47.

Garner, S. Paul. "Highlights in the Development of Cost Accounting," *The National Public Accountant,* March 1950, pp. 2-14.

Hawley, Frederick B. "Reply to Final Objections to the Risk Theory of Profits," *Quarterly Journal of Economics,* August 1901, pp. 603-20.

Horrigan, James O. "A Short History of Financial Ratio Analysis," *Accounting Review,* April 1968, pp. 284-94.

Hoxsey, J. M. B. "Accounting for Investors," *Journal of Accountancy,* October 1930, pp. 251-84.

Jennings, Alvin R. "Accounting Research," *Accounting Review,* October 1958, pp. 547-54.

Kohler, Eric L. "Tendencies in Balance Sheet Construction," *Accounting Review,* December 1926, pp. 1-11.

Littleton, A. C. "Principles of Valuation as Related to the Balance Sheet," *Papers and Proceedings of the Eighth Annual Meeting,* American Association of University Instructors in Accounting, 1923, pp. 14-15.

———. "Value and Price in Accounting," *Accounting Review,* September 1929, pp. 147-54.

May, George O. "Accounting Concepts and Standards Underlying Corporate Financial Statements," *Journal of Accountancy,* November 1948, pp. 56-61.

———. "Authoritative Financial Accounting," *Journal of Accountancy,* August 1946, pp. 102-19.

———. "Business Income," *The Accountant,* September 30, 1950, pp. 315-23.

———. "Improvements in Financial Accounts," *Journal of Accountancy,* May 1937, pp. 333-69.

———. "Taxable Income and Accounting Bases for Determining It," *Journal of Accountancy,* October 1925, pp. 248-66.

Miller, Herbert E. "The 1948 Revision of the American Accounting Association's Statement of Principles—A General Appraisal," *Accounting Review,* January 1949, pp. 44-50.

Paton, William A. "Recent and Prospective Developments in Accounting Theory." In *Selected Readings in Accounting and Auditing,* edited by Mary E. Murphy. New York: Prentice-Hall, 1952.

———. "Valuation of Inventories," *Journal of Accountancy,* December 1922, pp. 432-50.

Peloubet, M. E. "Depreciation Under the Revenue Act of 1934," *Journal of Accountancy,* September 1934, pp. 169-97.

Phillips, Edward G. "The Accretion Concept of Income," *Accounting Review,* January 1963, pp. 14-25.

Sanders, T. H. "Influence of the Securities and Exchange Commission upon Accounting Principles," *Accounting Review,* March 1936, pp. 66-74.

Smart, Jackson W. "Public Accounting Practice in the United States with Particular Reference to Current Problems," *The Accountant,* August 14, 1948, pp. 129-35.

Sprouse, Robert T. "Accounting for What-You-May-Call-Its," *Journal of Accountancy,* October 1966, pp. 45-53.

Taylor, J. R. "Some Antecedents of the Securities and Exchange Commission," *Accounting Review,* June 1941, pp. 188-96.

Thompson, C. Bertrand. "The Literature of Scientific Management," *Quarterly Journal of Economics,* June 1914, pp. 506-57.

Vance, Lawrence. "The Authority of History in Inventory Valuation," *Accounting Review,* July 1943, pp. 219-27.

Walker, Francis. A. "The Source of Business Profits," *The Quarterly Journal of Economics,* April 1887, pp. 265-88.

Whitmore, John. "Factory Accounts as Applied to Machine Shops," *Journal of Accountancy,* August 1906 and November 1906, pp. 248-58, 106-14.

Windal, Floyd W. "The Accounting Concept of Realization," *Accounting Review,* April 1961, pp. 249-58.

Yamey, Basil S. "Accounting and the Rise of Capitalism: Further Notes on a Theme by Sombart," *Journal of Accounting Research,* Autumn 1964, pp. 117-36.

PUBLIC DOCUMENTS

Eisner v. *Macomber,* 252 (U. S.) 183 (1920).

Securities and Exchange Commission, "Release No. 70; Revision of Regulation S-X," *Accounting Series Releases.* Washington: U. S.

Government Printing Office, 1956.

U. S. Government. *Mimeograph 4170 Revised,* 1936.

U. S. Government. *Regulation 45.* (1918) Article 1582.

U. S. Government. *Revenue Act of 1918.* Section 214 (a-7) .

U. S. Government. *Revenue Act of 1924.* Section 204 (c) .

U. S. Government. *Securities Act of 1933.* An act of May 27, 1933.

U. S. Government. *Securities Exchange Act of 1934.* An act of June 6, 1934.

U. S. Government. *Underwood-Simmons Tariff Law.* (1913) , Reg. 23.

U. S. Government. *Verification of Financial Statements (Revised).* Washington: U.S. Government Printing Office, 1929.

U. S. Securities and Exchange Commission. *Accounting Series Releases.* Washington: U. S. Government Printing Office.

Other publications in the accounting field:

THE ACCOUNTING CONCEPT OF REALIZATION
  Floyd W. Windal
        Paper 90 pp. 1961 $2.50

ACCOUNTING FOR HUMAN ASSETS
  Roger H. Hermanson
        Paper 69 pp. 1964 $2.50

CASH MOVEMENTS ANALYSIS OF THE ACCOUNTING
FOR CORPORATE INCOME TAXES
  Hugo Nurnberg
        Paper 182 pp. 1971 $6.25

THE CHECKLESS SOCIETY: ITS COST
IMPLICATIONS FOR THE FIRM
  William H. Mateer
        Cloth 129 pp. 1969 $7.00

CONTRIBUTIONS OF FOUR ACCOUNTING PIONEERS:
KOHLER, LITTLETON, MAY, PATON
  James Don Edwards and Roland F. Salmonson
        Cloth 238 pp. 1961 $7.50

THE EFFECTS OF DATA PROCESSING SERVICE BUREAUS
ON THE PRACTICE OF PUBLIC ACCOUNTING
  Constantine Konstans
        Cloth 205 pp. 1968 $7.00

THE EVOLUTION OF CPA ETHICS:
A PROFILE OF PROFESSIONALIZATION
  Darwin J. Casler
        Paper 139 pp. 1964 $2.50

DIVISION OF RESEARCH
5 J BERKEY HALL
GRADUATE SCHOOL OF BUSINESS ADMINISTRATION
MICHIGAN STATE UNIVERSITY
EAST LANSING, MICHIGAN